Ask Me Anything

MY TRANSPARENT
TRANSITION STORY

Jennifer Marie

ASK ME ANYTHING

MY TRANSPARENT TRANSITION STORY

JENNIFER MARIE

For more information: visit https://www.jennspire.com/contact

ISBN (Paperback):978-1-962280-55-6
ISBN (eBook):978-1-962280-56-3

Contents

Letter from the Author

To All the Haters,

I know by writing this book that I will receive hundreds if not thousands of hate messages for putting all of myself out there. I really hope you will read this book as I wrote it for people who struggle with understanding transgender people and the other pieces of the gender spectrum. If you are still so closed minded that you cannot do that, I feel sorry for you.

I feel sorry that you are closed off to understanding something so complicated as my beautiful transgender community. I am also sorry that you think Jesus would want you to act this way toward anyone. I have a personal relationship with Jesus myself and I can tell you that He is love, not hate.

When you write to me, and I know you will, just know that I will be deleting your message and not responding to it in any way. I know exactly who I am, I am proud of it, and I am proud of my resilient transgender community. Many of us have been through more in our lives than you can even imagine, and we made it through. We are resilient and we are loved.

LOVE WINS!

-Jenn

Acknowledgements

I would not be where I am without my amazing family. All of you have and continue to support me, and for that I am extremely grateful. I am blessed to have such a great family!

In addition to my amazing family, I wouldn't be here without my friends. Old friends and new, you are my chosen family and your support means the world. Some of you even helped with my coming out, my book, my business, and my website; I am grateful for everything!

A special thanks to my social media family. You all helped carry me when I couldn't share what was really going on. I will never forget your support.

Next, I want to thank all of the people who don't understand this complicated life that is being transgender. Whether you are trying to understand or not, I wrote this book for you! I know how difficult all of this is to understand. I have been there, as for many years I looked down on transgender people and the entire LGBTQIA+ community as a whole. But it's easy to look down on something you don't understand. I hope as you read this book, you will try to be as open as possible. I am not asking you to agree with me. I'm asking that you treat all people with respect.

This book would not be what it is without the help of my team at Big Idea to Bestseller. I have never written a book before, and never thought I would, but when I needed help making this dream come true, God answered.

One day I was having coffee with Megan Reed, who I had been recently introduced to as she is also a life coach, speaker, and writer. She wrote a book called *Main Character Energy*. (If you are looking to get out of your own way to accomplish something big in your life, I highly recommend it!) That morning Megan and I met for the first time, through a mutual friend. I told her all about my business and she told me about hers. One of the best things I left from that conversation with Megan was to follow a guy named Jake Kelfer (@jakekelfer) on Instagram.

I followed Jake and soon learned that he has a business that can help you with all of the various stages of your book. Jake and I talked and he was very supportive of my book and what it was going to do, so we put together a plan. After I finished writing my book, I wanted help with flow, editing, layout, design, publishing, launch and more. Jake's team helped me with all of those things.

I especially want to thank Miriam, who has not only written her own books, but helped hundreds of authors with theirs. Miriam was so passionate about my book and what it would do for thousands of people that she gave my story a lot of extra attention refining and suggesting some crucial missing pieces that helped make this story what it is.

And lastly, I want to thank you for buying this book. I can't wait to share my story with you!

Introduction

"You're like a butterfly . . . it is born and lives a good portion of its life as a caterpillar, and then it transforms and becomes something really beautiful."

— My Cousin Kim

If you're looking for the most common story of a trans woman who from the day they were born pretty much knew that they were born in the wrong body, then this isn't for you. This is my story. The story of the transgender woman that you do not really hear about. Each of us has our own journey, and there's no right or wrong way to be trans.

Over the years I have added to and revised my story so many times, but the first time I wrote it, I wrote it to connect with a community of people like me, and to share in hopes that someone would find comfort in knowing that they are not alone. I never dreamed of the response that I would get; all of the amazing people that have reached out to me have given me fuel to expand my story and share it with you!

As you read my story, I want it to feel personal because it is very personal to me. I've shared a hundred different versions of this story before I came out. Each time was different, as different things applied to the conversations I was having with each of those individuals. It is why I wrote this in such a way that you can imagine me sitting next to you sharing my story with you bearing my entire soul, and asking for nothing in return. Some people may not like that, and that is okay. If that is you, you can stop reading now.

I also want to share with you from the beginning that I am a Christian and I will not hide it. I will not try to convert you as I tell you my story, but it will be in my story multiple times, as it is one of the biggest parts of who I am. If you are not okay with that, you can stop reading now.

If you are still with me, you are in for a ride as my journey has been a roller coaster. There are ups and downs, twists and turns, and you may experience a whole range of different emotions, but I can almost guarantee you will have a smile on your face at the end!

Chapter One

Childhood

I was born in 1985 as the first child of two very loving, Christian parents. They both took great care of me.

My earliest memories are few and far between. My first memory is after my sister was born, when I was about three; I was feeding her a bottle of formula. It made her happy, so I knew I loved holding and taking care of her.

My sister and I had a great childhood. The two of us were always playing together. We were all very close with my grandparents, especially Mom's parents. They lived a couple hours away, but we would go visit them frequently, or they would come visit us.

When I was about four years old, we were visiting my grandparents and I was snooping—something I did quite often. I was opening every drawer I could until I stumbled upon a silk pink nightgown and robe. I instantly enjoyed touching it lightly with my fingers as it was so soft. I do not remember how I ended up putting it on, but I vividly remember that when I did, I immediately loved the way it made me feel!

Each time we went to visit my grandparents, every couple months or so, I would sneak away and carefully open the drawer that held the pink robe and nightgown, put it on, and wear it around as I played. It was all fun and games until later that year I was told by my parents, "It's not funny anymore, and you need to stop." I remember my heart sinking into the bottom of my chest . . . I don't think I ever tried it on again. I now can look back on that moment and realize I wanted so badly to share with my family what I was feeling, but their immediate shut-down made me retreat. I buried those feelings deep down that day.

Shortly after that, I found my mother's and aunt's old dresses in my grandparents' basement, and I loved looking at them. They were so pretty! I knew I had to wear them! I couldn't *not* try them on, actually. Whenever I got the chance, I would sneak downstairs and try them on in secret.

No one ever caught me. I had some close calls where I had to take them off quickly, but I had my clothes on underneath, so it was easy to change. (I continued to try them on until I eventually outgrew them, around age fifteen.)

Elementary School Memories

One magical day when I was about six years old, my sister received a dress-up box for her third birthday. There were all kinds of dresses and skirts in it. I remember at first just looking at them, and holding them as much as I could without raising suspicions.

Unfortunately, most of the clothes were too small for me, until out of the blue Mom found some old dresses of hers and added them to the box. My heart started racing! They were so feminine and beautiful, and I couldn't wait to try them on!

Over the years, either my sister would dress me up or I would make her a bet or dare, to somehow *get* her to get me to dress up. We always had fun with it. I remember doing it one time when my best friend, who was a boy, was having a sleepover at my house; my sister dressed both of us up, and we had a great time. My parents thought it was funny, especially because he was dressed up, too.

While I had a great family, not everyone else around me was as kind to me during those years. I attended the upper middle class school in the district, and many of the kids were mean to me. I was never a very masculine kid; I didn't have a backbone and was terrible at comebacks, so kids always picked on me. I remember getting sick of it so much there were years that when school was out, I sat at home without friends. The only positive was it gave me more opportunities to play dress up.

Some of them joked that I was gay. I remember sitting at home, thinking, *Am I gay?* By the time I was a preteen, I knew that I liked girls and was attracted to them . . . and I was not at all attracted to guys. I loved girls, but I also loved dressing up. So then I thought, *Maybe I'm a lesbian trapped inside a man's body?* I thought that thought was kind of funny, and even made up a silly song about it, likely a defense mechanism to hide the truth from myself.

The First Halloween

One year in late elementary school, I remember hearing about one of our friends who dressed up as a grandma for Halloween. I remember thinking how fun that would be to dress (It is common to just say "to dress" instead of say crossdress) and be in public without people thinking too much about it. When Mom asked me what I wanted to be for Halloween, I mentioned the guy that dressed as a grandma, and that it sounded like fun.

She immediately went to the dress-up box and picked out a beautiful burgundy dress, and a green skirt with a matching green blouse. She got some pantyhose out of her drawer and helped me put them on, along with the dress. To accessorize, she gave me her short blonde wig from her childhood and clip-on earrings, then helped me put them on. After I was fully dressed, including the wig and accessories, she went to her makeup drawer and applied some eyeshadow, blush, and lipstick. I remember feeling butterflies like I had never felt—I was loving every second!

We took some photos in the burgundy dress, and then she helped me put on the green skirt and matching top. After a few more photos, Mom said it was time to take it all off. I didn't want it to end, but did as I was told—I did not want to raise any suspicions of how much I liked this. I never had a Halloween party to go to that year, so I didn't wear them again . . . except in secret.

https://www.jennspire.com/1-my-first-halloween

Middle School Memories

Middle school came around, and I made a few friends. I remember one special day I went with my friend's church group to a baseball game. On the way out of the game, it was pouring rain. We were all drenched. When we got back to the church, everyone put on clothes from a dress-up box the youth group had while our clothes dried. I remember seeing a beautiful, long, light-blue dress.

After everyone had changed into something from the dress-up box and had left the room, I grabbed the dress I couldn't take my eyes off of and put it on. When I walked out of the room into the other room where everyone was playing, everyone laughed about it for a minute, and then we just played games like hide and seek. No one said anything else about it the rest of the night.

Around midnight, it was time to go to sleep and our clothes were dry, so I took off the dress. Even though I didn't want it to end, I put on my regular clothes and went to sleep.

Getting Caught!

In my late middle school years, Mom came home early one day, and I was in our basement wearing one of the dresses from the dress-up box. When I heard her open the door upstairs, I was so scared, I felt like I was about to jump out of my skin. Since I had started dressing at home, I found it was more fun to wear only my underwear under the clothes (which meant it took longer to change).

She called for me, asking where I was, and I did not answer. As she came down the basement stairs, I walked out of the bathroom. With my heart pounding, I had taken everything off as fast as possible, put the dress under the bathroom sink, and closed the bathroom door. She knew something was up, as I was completely flustered. I never could tell a lie, especially to Mom; when she asked what I was doing, I replied, "Nothing."

She knew I was not telling her the truth.

I finally broke down crying, after holding this secret for so many years, and told her I had been sneaking around and wearing girls' clothes in secret. It was a weight lifted off my shoulders to finally tell someone, but also terrifying . . . because I did not know what she would do with this information. I made her promise not to tell Dad, and later confirmed she had kept my secret all these years. The one condition she had to not tell Dad was that I would see a therapist. I agreed, so she took me to a family counselor.

The days I went to talk to the counselor, I was so nervous. We talked about a lot of things, but I never could get the courage to tell him about my dressing. I know counselors are supposed to be understanding and not judge, but at the time I felt like a freak. I did not want the judgment or weird looks, so I kept my mouth closed on that topic.

Because I shared a lot of other personal things, I didn't think the counselor thought I was hiding anything. I was in denial; I was so sure it was just about clothes that I thought leaving that part out was fine. After the series of sessions, Mom and I didn't talk much about it either, which was a huge relief.

High School Memories

When it came time for high school, most of my friends left to go to private school. It was difficult, because I had worked so hard to make friends in school and now they were leaving me. I knew I had to start over. I was attracted to one of the girls in my band section, so I invited myself along to a hangout with her and her friends. I joined her group, and we had great times together.

Years later, two of the guys in this group of friends came out as gay. Even though I knew I loved wearing women's clothes, and thought about it constantly my entire life, never in a million years would I have thought I was part of LGBTQIA+ like them. I knew I wasn't gay—I was attracted to girls, I just had this other *thing*, another part of me that I kept to myself.

Looking back on it all, I now know I never let myself explore my feminine side. There are two reasons for this. One, back in those days I was a very introverted, quiet, reserved person. The other reason was religion, but the shocking thing is it wasn't even my church. I grew up Methodist, where they focused on loving your neighbor and focusing on your own personal relationship with God. The problem was all the other religious groups I joined. I will not name any of them, but they all had Baptist or other evangelistic backgrounds. Being part of these groups was powerful, because their message was powerful, and they are great at getting people hyped up. I still believe there is a lot of good that they do, but there is also a lot of harm that I experienced.

Throughout my life, at their various events, there was one common thread that caused the most damage: the mindset that you must take everything you read in the Bible at face value, and not question anything. I now know that asking questions can allow you to grow deeper in your faith.

The other very harmful thing was the way and number of times I was told being LGBT is a sin. Now I believe people have a right to believe what they want to, but please don't cast judgment on someone else for what they believe.

This was all so damaging to little Jenn who was buried deep inside me. Back then, I never challenged anything in my life. I was the definition of a follower, even beyond the biblical sense. I did what I was told, so I didn't question and just believed whatever I was told to believe. I cast a lot of secret judgment on LGBT people, and at the same time, covered up Jenn with more dirt when she was already buried from my childhood. Looking back on it, I had no idea what I was doing at that time, as I was just going with the flow

24

and not questioning anything (just as my training had taught me); remember, I was in complete denial.

Hookers and Little Miss Muffet

Sophomore year of high school was my first opportunity to dress up publicly in years. My marching-band friends and I were discussing Halloween, and someone joked that we should go as "hookers." (No, I would not use that term now, but that is what we said back then.) While my heart raced, I smiled and said, "Let's do it!" So, we did.

I wore my girlfriend's short spaghetti-strap gray dress with black butterflies on it, a shoulder-length brown wig that Mom and I bought from a costume shop, black fishnets, strappy high heels Mom and I purchased at Payless, and stuffed the top of the dress with socks.

My girlfriend's mother put heavy makeup on me. It was the first time I had worn mascara, and my eyelashes kept fluttering so much it felt like they were about to fly away. But I loved it! We took some pictures of me walking down the stairs, then I was handed a bag, and we were off to trick-or-treat.

We were way too old (we were in high school, for crying out loud) but we thought it would be funny . . . and I wasn't going to pass up an outing dressed up like this. This was the first time in my life that I felt sexy dressed as a woman. When people opened their doors to the three of us, some didn't know what our costumes were, and others didn't even know we were not girls. It was so much fun!

Before I had agreed to dress as a "hooker" with my friends for Halloween, my girlfriend and I had decided to go as Little Miss Muffet and the spider—with me, of course, as Little Miss Muffet. I most likely mentioned I thought it would be funny. Mom and I went to the thrift store to find a dress. I tried on a few until we settled on a beautiful pink one with cap sleeves, a large full skirt and a bow on the back. I was thrilled, as it was so girly; I thought it would be perfect.

Unfortunately, my girlfriend's mother also bought a dress. Her dress was a short blue gingham, and she bought pantaloons, because that was the picture she had of what Little Miss Muffet wore in the story. I liked my dress better, but my girlfriend's mother was adamant with her selection, so I went with her outfit. I wore her dress, pantaloons, white tights, Mom's white slippers, and the same brown wig but with a bonnet my girlfriend's mother had made. They applied a little blush, eyeshadow, and lipstick. Finally, my girlfriend, dressed as the spider, and I were off.

When I walked in the door at the party, no one knew who I was until they saw my girlfriend . . . and then they did a double-take. They laughed when they figured out it was me. We voted on awards for several categories. I had hoped I would win "cutest costume," but when I was voted "scariest costume," I was so disappointed; I didn't want it to be a joke, because it wasn't a joke to me. I played it off well, and accepted my award with a smile on my face.

As a consolation, I remember being excited because now I had *two dresses* of my own: the beautiful pink dress I'd wanted to wear to the party, and the blue gingham one I actually wore.

The dresses were kept in the attic, just down the hall from my bedroom. When Mom and I were putting them away, my sister passed by the attic and asked what we were doing. Mom told her we were putting the Halloween dresses away, and then showed my sister and I some of her old dresses, including her wedding dress. She mentioned my sister could wear it sometime if she wanted to. I remember wishing on the inside that she would ask me if I wanted to wear it, but that time never came. But at least I did learn about several dresses stored up there that I hoped would fit me . . . and I could not wait to find out.

There were two dresses in that attic that I really loved. Both had long sleeves. One was a long red dress, and the other was what I thought of as a "Little House on the Prairie" dress. It was a long dress with long sleeves. The top was red, and the attached skirt was a red and white gingham check with a tie on the back. Both dresses zipped up. Every time I was home alone, I would sneak into the attic and pull on at least one of those dresses, reaching for the back to pull up that zipper. They were "my" dresses.

https://www.jennspire.com/2-hookersandlittlemissmuffet

Dressing with the Band

I only recall one significant moment from my junior year of high school. As I mentioned earlier, I was in the marching band, and I enjoyed it. I even marched on the front line of the Rose Bowl Parade in my sophomore year.

During summer band camp my junior year, one of the guys thought it would be funny for all of us to wear dresses during band practice for one day. I told Mom, and she asked one of our family friends to borrow a dress. I wore an old-school prom dress that was black and had beautiful sequins. I don't believe I wore a wig, but Mom had applied a little makeup before I left. When I arrived, I found that only a couple other guys were dressed up and none had on makeup. Despite some of the comments I got, including from the band director, I found joy in it and had a good time, as I was dressed how I wanted to be.

Senior Year

I was in the marching band until the end of my junior year. I had played trombone since middle school and while I liked it, I wanted to experience high school outside of the band. I wanted to sit in the stands at the football stadium with the rest of the students. When I was finally able to, I had expected to watch the football game, but I usually just sat in the bleachers wishing I was a cheerleader wearing one of those cute skirts, cheering on the team.

My friends and I waited until we were seniors before we started drinking. We were all smart and did not want to get in any trouble, so each time we drank we stayed overnight at the house we were at. No one ever left the basement until morning. I remember at one of our first parties someone made a joke that they saw one of our guy friends sneak off and caught him wearing one of the host's mother's dresses. Even though they were just joking and totally made the entire thing up, I remember chuckling outside, but on the inside thinking, *Thank heavens no one is making that joke about me. I don't want them to know my secret.*

https://www.jennspire.com/3-hs-senior-year

Chapter Two

Young Adulthood

I left for my freshman year of college excited for the "best time of your life" years, but still the same confused kid with a huge secret that I couldn't share with anyone. The only difference was now I didn't have anything to dress up in, so I did not dress again until Halloween. Months had gone by, and I was constantly thinking about Halloween and how rapidly it was approaching. When I talked openly about not knowing what I should be for Halloween, my friend suggested I go as a Playboy Bunny, as a joke of course. I said, "Challenge accepted."

I went down to the local Halloween store and walked right in with my heart pounding. The owner was wearing a Playboy Bunny costume. It was a short pink dress with a fluffy white tail and white fur above the breasts and of course the Playboy Bunny ears and cuffs. When he asked what I wanted, I told him I needed a Playboy Bunny costume, just like he was wearing.

"Will you need white fishnets, too?" he asked.

"Of course," I replied. He rang them up and I went back to the dorm room.

I went out shopping with a girlfriend and bought white high heels. They were backless, so they were very challenging to walk in and hurt my feet, but I still loved every minute! A couple girls in the dorm heard what I was doing and got excited. One loaned me a pink wig and they did my makeup. It was such a fun experience, except for those heels. They were terrible to walk in; the heel flapped with every step I took. The only part of the night I found funny was when we saw another college girl at the party that was wearing the same costume. Someone mentioned that I wore it better and she got all in a tizzy!

Beautiful Woman

Sophomore year of college . . . while I may not recall every specific incident, I do know that I spent a lot of time convincing others into daring or challenging me to dress up. As I reflect back on everything now, I now understand why I was always trying to convince people to dare or challenge me this way; in fact, I believe it is a result of two things.

With it all being so taboo and knowing I couldn't tell anyone the truth, I am sure one of my ways of hiding the truth from myself was by convincing myself if someone else thought it was fun, then it would be fine for me. I would not have any shame associated with it if it was someone else's idea.

I also just always wanted an excuse to be out and about as a woman. Halloween was my excuse for that, so I took almost every opportunity I could. No one ever said anything negative when I dressed up as a result of a lost bet, dare, or challenge . . . so I did it a lot.

Sophomore year for Halloween I went as a *beautiful* woman—not a "hooker," not a nursery rhyme character, not as a sexual object—I wanted to be a glamorous, sophisticated woman, like you'd see in old movies from the 1940s and 1950s. I went with a friend to the thrift store and bought a long dark red formal dress. It had some crinoline at the bottom which made me feel prettier than ever.

I remember telling Mom what I was doing and asked her if I could have the brown wig and high heels with straps that I wore in high school. I had to ask a couple times. She told me she couldn't find the wig, but gave me the shoes. Before she handed them over, she said, "I know we haven't talked about that for a while. How are you doing with all of that?"

"Oh, I am all done with that. This is just for fun," I lied. This is one of only a couple times I remember blatantly lying to her. I did not want her to worry, and I was concerned how she would react if she knew it was still affecting me . . . so I lied.

I was terrified of going wig shopping by myself and really wanted someone to know my secret, so I told my ex-girlfriend I liked to dress as a girl sometimes. She agreed to go shopping with me for my Halloween costume. We went to a wig store, and I remember wanting a light blonde wig. I hinted at one in particular, but obviously she didn't know which one I meant. She told the clerk we wanted the one next to it—a dirty-blonde wig. I was so nervous to say anything, so I just accepted it and paid for it, even though it wasn't the sort of look I was going for. We went to Walmart to buy black panties and pantyhose. It was the first time I had any of my own. Another friend offered to help me with my wig and makeup.

She cut the wig to add swooping bangs and applied full makeup, more makeup than I had ever worn. She even gave me smokey eyes! Then she pulled out some cute dangly clip-on earrings that she had purchased for me at the accessories store she worked at. I felt beautiful! People told me I was pretty; they smiled or laughed, and then pretty much acted normal. I liked a little bit of attention, but deep down, I just wanted to be one of the girls.

Later that year—several times when my dorm mates were gone—I pulled out my box from under my bed and put on my Halloween costume from earlier in the year with the dark red gown, panties, hose, heels, and wig. I was terrified someone would walk in at any minute, so much so that I didn't ever stay dressed long, especially after I heard people in the hall.

This was also the same year that I convinced another one of my friends to dress me up. She was a pretty girl and lived in a townhouse by herself. We knew each other only because we used to work together. I suggested we hang out, and after dinner, I somehow convinced her it would be funny to dress me up. She was not enthused, but at my persistence, we went to her closet. I remembered this cute floral skirt and top she would wear. I saw it immediately, and made my way around the closet until I settled back on my selection. I put it on, and I got the feeling she did not think it was funny. After a few minutes of awkwardness I took it all off, hung out for a few minutes more, and she did not seem to be in a good mood, so I left.

I never saw her again.

https://www.jennspire.com/4-beautifulwoman

Junior Year

Junior year, I moved into my own studio apartment. I did not dress up as a girl for Halloween, but it was a great year as I lived on my own. This was the first year I could dress whenever I wanted to and not have to worry about someone walking in on me. I dressed *a lot* that year. I am sure the guy that lived below me probably thought I had a lot of girls visiting who liked to wear heels. The only thing I regret was not getting more clothes and buying makeup so I could start to learn how to style myself and begin the difficult process of learning how to apply makeup.

Sorority Girl

Senior year, I continued to dress whenever I wanted to, as I still lived alone. My friend who attended a university in another part of the state mentioned that if I did not have anything to do for Halloween that I should come visit her. I asked her what I should dress as for Halloween. After I shot down several of her ideas, she joked and said I could be her sorority sister. I asked what they wore, and she said red. I went out and bought a short red dress with a low-cut v-neck.

When I went to see her, she mentioned she also had a French maid costume she had worn one year, and that I could try it, too. It was so cute and a fantasy of mine, so of course I tried it on. We both agreed it was *way* too small on me, so I wore the red dress, pantyhose, heels, and wig I had brought with me. She applied full makeup, and we were off to party-hop. My friend could really drink, but until that night I had no idea how *much more* she could drink than me.

I tried to keep up with her. When she drank, I drank. I drank so much that night, it still remains one of the only times in my life that I actually blacked out. All I remember from that night was drinking jungle juice, talking to a guy at one of the houses (later, I heard that he was flirting with me), laying on the grass in "the quad," puking in her friend's car, and stumbling into my friend's dorm room. Definitely *not* my finest moment!

I woke up still dressed with makeup on my face lying on the floor. I thanked my friend for taking care of me, apologized for my drunken behavior, and drove back to my college campus. I continued to dress frequently in my own apartment until I moved home.

Dating

From fifth grade on, I usually had a girlfriend, but the first girlfriend I actually asked out on a date did not come until my sophomore year of high school. I was so shy that girls always asked *me* out. . .

that is, until Lucy. Lucy was in the choir. She had long brown hair and I thought she was really pretty. She was also the first girl I ever kissed. I was so awkward about it, too. In the end, it felt like she got bored with me and was rude, so I had to break up with her because yes, I was that sensitive.

Looking back on it now, I was mostly interested in Lucy because she was the girl I wanted to be, or at least *thought* I wanted to be. She was pretty, had long hair like I probably deep down always wanted, and she was a little awkward, like me.

I dated several girls over the years and when I wasn't dating, I was making out with just about every girl I could. I even joked and called myself a "make-out slut."

Toward the end of college, my life changed when I reconnected with a friend from childhood. We had known each other since I was about seven, as our families were close. One week when we were both home from school, we went out as friends. I remember her opening the door and I could not stop thinking how beautiful she was. Her hair was long and curled, her makeup was perfect, and she was dressed cute with nice accessories. The second she opened the door I started having feelings that I never had about her before. Even though we had known each other for many years, and I had even taken her as my date to homecoming (as friends), I knew that things were now very different for me.

We went to dinner and then to see the movie *Juno*, of all movies, but we both thought it looked funny and cute. Soon after, I decided to visit her at her school. We went to the theater to see *Forgetting*

Sarah Marshall, and then returned to her apartment. We stayed up until 5:00 a.m., just talking on her couch. I knew I had to take things slowly because our parents were friends, and I did not want to mess that up. For the next several months, I called her every time I was driving home or driving back to school, just to "pass the time" . . . or so I told her. I was truly in love with her, so shortly after we started officially dating and a couple years later, I asked her to marry me.

Crossdressing in Front of My Future Wife

While my girlfriend and I were dating—before we were engaged—I was having the urge to dress with her. I realize now I was just trying to be myself. It wasn't that I needed an excuse anymore, as I was living alone in my little studio apartment, so I could dress whenever I wanted to. She had become my best friend and the love of my life. I now realize I wanted to share everything with her, including this part of me.

One time, we were talking about how she loved the movie *Little Women*. I had never seen the movie, and I convinced her to dress me up and watch it together. She did not bring any clothes for me, but I told her I had dressed as a woman for Halloween before, so I had a dress. She got out her makeup, and tried leaving me to do it myself; I had no idea what I was doing, as I had never used makeup on my own. I applied a couple of things, and asked for her help. She did not seem to have fun with it, but applied makeup to my face. I put on my dark red formal dress, and we sat on my futon and watched the movie.

I remember loving the movie, but I also remember I felt like she was pissed about it the entire night. I tried snuggling up to her and even tried kissing her. She refused both. She informed me that she was *not* attracted to women, and that there was no way she was kissing me tonight. I felt completely rejected, and knew that I could not share with her what I was really feeling. I had never felt so calm in my body and tortured by someone's reaction in my life.

Now, I look back on that experience and realize that horrible night was a wake-up call; I knew in my heart I couldn't share my deepest secret with her, at least not yet.

Coming Out to My Fiancée

After college, I moved home and lived in my childhood bedroom. For the few months I was back home, there was no opportunity to dress; when I finally moved into a townhouse by myself, I was able to dress occasionally. And when I did, I had to find time when my fiancée was not around.

Before we got married, I did what I thought was the right thing to do and told her that I liked dressing as a woman. One of her favorite comedians was Eddie Izzard; at the time, Eddie identified as a transvestite[1] who did not hide it at all. I told her I was kind of like Eddie.

She asked me if that meant that I liked wearing women's clothes.

---

1. For clarity purposes, a *transvestite* is an old term which means a person who dresses in clothes of the opposite gender. The term is now considered offensive, so now we just say crossdresser. Eventually, Eddie came out as transgender.

"Unfortunately, yes." I replied.

She seemed to go through a whirlwind of emotions from our conversations that week. From asking if I could dress only on Halloween to not being sure whether she could continue with our relationship, her questions and comments amounted to one hell of a week for the two of us.

Many years later, she indicated she really was about to break up over it, and thinks maybe she should have. But back then, we both saw it as a problem that I needed to work on and since we were in love, we stayed together.

Wedding Day

We got married right before I turned twenty-six. I remember waking up the day of our wedding and it felt completely different than I ever imagined. I was marrying the girl of my dreams; why could I not be completely happy? My entire life I had dreamed of wearing a wedding dress, and it was all coming back to me harder than ever! I proceeded to throw some clothes on and head to the church.

When I arrived, all I could think about was wanting to wear the wedding dress the entire day. *I* wanted to be the bride, and have pictures taken with *me* in the dress. I remember her complaining about how hard it was to get up and down and pose in all of those ways in that heavy gown. I kept thinking, "I would give anything to be in your shoes! Trade places with me!"

I was a mess, and I could tell my fiancée knew something was off, but I never let her know the reason why. The week before our wedding, I had received a terrible haircut from my stylist. I would not admit I did not like the haircut, and both of our mothers kept trying to fix it and kept making comments. I let her think that was what was bothering me, and why I was not myself. The truth is I knew my haircut had hardly anything to do with it. I wanted to be the bride and it was killing me to not be!

We made it through the ceremony and pictures, and then I got some food and alcoholic beverages . . . so I was doing a little better. I had a great time dancing with my bride and our friends, even though I continued thinking I wanted to be wearing the dress.

At the end of the night, we made it to the newlywed suite at our hotel. I had trouble performing, so we did not consummate the marriage that night. Honestly, I had trouble with performing our entire marriage. It should have been easy, but we had to practice a lot for it to be right. I never knew why—that is, until many years later.

Looking back on this, I never should have gotten married before I had worked through everything I was feeling inside, and I would like to think if the resources that are available now had been available then, I would have. I truly believe I was in love with her, and everything in our marriage was real. We had a lot of great times together, but we both also experienced a lot of heartache as well.

Chapter Three

Early Marriage

Before we get into the heart of what happened after I got married, I want to explain a couple topics that may be difficult for people to fully understand. It is impossible to comprehend without experiencing these feelings, but I am going to do my best to give you insight.

Up to this point, I have shown you all kinds of examples of how, throughout my entire life, I was constantly thinking about presenting as a woman—so much that I used every means available to present how I wanted to. Whether I was convincing someone, dressing when any gender-bending opportunity might arise, or dressing up when no one was home, I found a way.

But why did I do this?

It took me many years to understand what was going on. The constant battles I was having with this urge and need to dress up was my gender dysphoria talking to me. So what exactly is *gender dysphoria*? The Mayo Clinic defines it in the following way:

> Gender dysphoria is the feeling of discomfort or distress that might occur in people whose gender identity differs from their sex assigned at birth or sex-related physical characteristics.[2]

My way of describing it is this constant feeling that something is not right within or on your body, and that manifests itself in your constant thoughts. It can cause your mood to change, you may become anxious, depressed, etc.

What I was experiencing as a kid was only a small portion of gender dysphoria. Why? Because I thought crossdressing was a sin, so I didn't dare take those thoughts beyond that. I was burying it all deep down inside and all I allowed to surface were the constant thoughts of wanting to dress as a woman. Continuously crossdressing served as my medicine. It gave me that feeling that I needed. What feeling was that? Gender euphoria!

So what is *gender euphoria*, then?

> Gender Euphoria is a proposed term for the opposite of gender dysphoria. It is the satisfaction, enjoyment, or relief felt by trans people when they feel their body matches their personal gender identity.[3]

---

2. "Gender Dysphoria - Symptoms and Causes - Mayo Clinic," 2024, Mayo Clinic, May 14, 2024, https://www.mayoclinic.org/diseases-conditions/gender-dysphoria/symptoms-causes/syc-20475255.

3. Contributors to Wikimedia projects. 2023, "Gender Euphoria," Simple English Wikipedia, the Free Encyclopedia. September 5, 2023, https://simple.wikipedia.org/wiki/Gender_euphoria#:~:text=Gender%20euphoria%20(GE)%20is%20a,the%20opposite%20of%20gender%20dysphoria.

The way I like to describe it as it relates to me is this calm and intense joy comes over me at the same time. Growing up, I was only experiencing a tiny bit of gender euphoria, but as I continue my journey you will see the intense joy that takes over my entire body.

Newlyweds

Shortly after we got married, I remember lying in bed one morning pretending to be sleeping while my wife was getting ready for work. I think she thought it would be funny to put makeup on me. She proceeded to put some light makeup on me while I continued to pretend to be sleeping (or at least pretended to be too tired to stop her).

I was loving every minute of it, so much that as soon as she was out the door, I ran to the bathroom to see. When I looked in the mirror, this natural smile came on my face. I applied a little bit more makeup, because I knew if I had any on me after I removed it, I could pass it off as the makeup she put on me. As soon as I was happy with it, I went to the closet and got out one of my old dresses from Halloween, put on my panties and pantyhose, stuffed the cups with socks, and completed the outfit with my heels and a wig. I looked in the mirror and liked the girl I saw looking back at me . . . so I stayed dressed for a couple hours and then removed it all so I would not get caught.

This Needs to Stop

I did not dress very much for the first three years of our marriage, but I also did not bring it up when I did, as it was never a pleasant conversation when we discussed it. By year four, I still had the desire to crossdress and we were trying to have a baby, so we both decided I needed to stop before the baby came. I laid out a plan to try to stop my dressing for good. It was all my idea. I was going to fully dress up for thirty days straight in the middle of the night. I really thought I could wear myself out of it, and hopefully not have the desire to do it again. As per my agreement with my wife, I would set my alarm to wake up in the middle of the night and put on my wig, apply full makeup I purchased at Dollar Tree, and try on all the outfits and accessories I purchased. I would then wear one outfit while I cleaned the house before I took it all off.

The first day I walked out of the bathroom dressed, our dog was terrified. She growled and barked at me, so I approached her to try to tell her who I was to calm her, but she attacked me. She was a relatively small dog, but her bite still drew blood. I scared the shit out of her, literally. My wife had to come settle her down so I could get back down to the basement to take it all off. I recall my wife and I having a conversation about how that reaction from our dog should make me want to stop. I got emotional, and told her I wanted to stop, but that was why I needed to continue. I continued the next night to try to make this desire stop for good.

Days went by, and it became daunting and exhausting. I was only getting three or four hours of sleep each night. I remember at times wishing I could take a night off as I was exhausted, but I powered through until the end.

It ended up taking forty-two days and I got an average of about three hours of sleep each night. It literally made me sick. I was hopeful that my desire to crossdress would fade. It did . . . but only for a couple weeks.

For the next five years, I dressed occasionally, typically only a few times a year when I had the house to myself for at least a couple hours. I even tried going to thrift stores in guy mode purchasing and then wearing a variety of different outfits in hopes I could ruin it for myself and rid myself of this desire. It obviously never worked.

https://www.jennspire.com/5-early-marriage-this-needs-to-stop

Birth of My Children

We had our first kid when I was thirty, about four years after we got married. I had always known I wanted to be a parent. From the time I was young, I loved kids and knew I wanted to have my own someday. Many trans women have dysphoria over not being able to birth children. I have never been like that. I wanted children and I have always been fine with not having carried them in my belly. But I know I wanted them so badly that if I had been born differently, there is not a doubt in my mind that I would have carried them.

My son was born in 2015. I knew I would love my kid but when he came, the intense emotions I had for him blew me away. I was so in love with him. I felt it deeply.

My daughter was born two years later, and I was complete. I had always wanted a son and a daughter and now I had one of each! My entire life when I pictured having a daughter, I dreamed of doing all kinds of feminine things with her. I imagined having her put makeup on me and dress me up, again I always felt it made it okay if someone feminized me. When she came, she had an instant sass, but a sweet and fun personality as well.

I was fully satisfied having two children since we had one of each. I was dying to get a vasectomy, so we didn't have any more. I waited several months until my wife gave me the go-ahead, and I had it done.

This *Really* Needs to Stop

In 2019, we had found a home that we could imagine with some elbow grease and love could be even better than a "dream home" either of us ever imagined. We purchased the house, and began the hard work to make it ours. Even though it was going to take months before we could move in, it had this unique charm about it that only exists in an older home. After some improvements on the first floor alone, we had a spacious master suite with a large bathroom, huge walk-in closet, a playroom, and a beautiful kitchen that opened up into a beautiful living room. The views were breathtaking.

My wife made it clear that she did not want my girl 'stuff' moving to the new house. I agreed. I did not want this to control my life either, but I also knew it would never work to fully purge everything (as I had heard so many people in my position tried to do) so I created a new plan. I would dress up in the basement whenever I could, and I would throw away one item every time I dressed. For the first few times, I threw away items I did not like or did not need anymore. After those were gone, I threw out a couple things I wanted, like some cute eyeglasses and earrings. It was after that, I knew I could not go on purging items. I was beginning to have anxiety over this; it was too much for me. I knew I could not continue, so I stopped.

When it was time to move to the new house, I secretly moved my items over in my car. My wife and I never discussed whether the items were gone; I did not want to create a fight, so I just moved them without discussing it. I knew exactly where to put them, because I noticed something while we were touring the house: contained inside one of the basement walls was a floor-to-ceiling hidden gun safe that was built out of wood and locked with a key. The key was in the lock. I knew that this is where my stuff could be stored safely from any prying eyes. I especially wanted it all to be discreet so my children would never find it. It was the perfect spot!

https://www.jennspire.com/6-early-marriage-this-really

Before the Move

Shortly before we were ready to move to the new house, my wife and the kids went on a weekend trip. As I had done my entire life when left alone, I seized the opportunity.

This time, I gathered my things and dressed up at the new house. There was no mirror on the wall, but that was not going to stop me. I leaned a mirror on the top of the vanity and applied makeup for the first time in the new house. I tried on several of my dresses and shoes, and took pictures. At the end of the night, I decided I was going to do something bold: I was going to drive to the old house dressed! No one was going to be there anyway, and it was only a fifteen-minute drive.

I carefully, quickly, and quietly loaded all of my items into the car that was sitting outside and opened my door, sat in the seat, carefully slid in my legs so as not to snag my stockings, and closed the door. My heart was pounding the entire way home. It was after 2:00 a.m., so there was hardly a car on the road. I remember one car passing me. I was so nervous even about that one car, but I just looked forward and kept driving. I pulled into our garage and shut the door. I had made it home safely!

I proceeded to our master bath and touched up my makeup. I took a few more pictures and then being that it was so late (almost 4:00 a.m.), I took it all off. Removing the makeup, taking off my high heels, slipping off the dress, undoing my bra and taking out my breast forms, removing the pantyhose but leaving on my panties, standing there looking in the mirror . . . between homes . . .

between versions of myself. What else could I do? I tucked it away back into the car and slid into the sheets.

https://www.jennspire.com/7-early-marriage-before

Chapter Four

Jenn Emerging

For as long as I had my own computer, I remember hopping online every few months to search crossdressing and related topics, but all I could find were stories of being forced to dress, made a bet and had to dress, magically turned into a woman, etc. I would read those stories to "take care" of myself in a "self-service act," because it made me stop thinking about it. Most men can tell you that "act" clears your mind, and that is exactly what it did for me.

Looking back, I did not understand my desire to dress. As a teenager—with all those hormones raging in my body—everything in a young man's life is about sex, so that is how I made sense of it, especially because that is all I could find online. The common theme in all the stories I liked was that it was out of the man's control. He was forced to turn into a woman, so it was not his fault. I wanted that to happen to me so badly, but life is not fantasy . . . and when I was reading those stories, I was living in a fantasy world.

On April 14, 2021, I searched the internet as usual, but this time I found a contest that Glamour Boutique was holding. It was a photo contest for crossdressers and transgender women. No one had ever seen my pictures of me all dressed up after applying my own makeup, so I was curious what they would think. After some internal debating, I decided to enter the contest. Best-case scenario, I would win a free breast plate, and worst-case scenario, it would go terribly, and I'd decide to never put myself out there ever again.

The contest entry appeared to be easier if done through Facebook. There was *no way* I was using my male account, so I decided to create a female account. I had never created a female name for myself before, so I had to think of one. It did not take me long to remember that I already had a name.

Growing up my sister would call me "Jennifer" when she dressed me up, and other times when she wanted to razz me for doing something girly. I always loved it, so I decided that *Jennifer* was it! I decided if I was going to put myself out there, I had to do it in a safe way so that none of my friends or family would be alerted or find my account. Here's how I did it, step-by-step:

- Created a new Google account.
- Created a Google Voice account with a new number.
- Created my new Facebook and made sure that when they asked for my phone number, I used Jennifer's new Google Voice number.

One nice thing I found was Google Voice has texting so I could set up two-factor authentication and have it text me on that Google Voice number when I logged in.

I started with a Facebook Lite app to keep it all separate, but soon grew paranoid that a notification would pop up or my wife or anyone else I handed my phone to would find my account or pictures on my phone. Instead of having to purchase and hide a burner phone for Jenn, I researched other solutions, and the best one did not cost me anything. It was right there on my phone all along: the Samsung Secure Folder app. At that time, that app allowed me to add apps and essentially create a whole new phone within my phone in a secure folder that was password protected. When I took pictures on my phone, I used the camera that was included within the secure folder, so my pictures stayed out of my main phone photos app. I backed them up to my Jennifer Google Photos account. I customized my secure folder and created Jenn's own special home on my phone.

After I had created my secure system, I entered the contest and explored a side of Facebook I was too nervous to ever think about exploring from my other account. I found a large community on Facebook and made a lot of friends very quickly. I created a home there, and loved the responses to the pictures I was posting. Finding community and having an outlet was a game-changer for me. While it would have been fun and super-affirming to win, I realized I did not care about winning the Glamour Boutique contest. I had found a second home online, and that felt like winning to me.

https://www.jennspire.com/8-jenn-emerging

Sharing My Story

April 2021 was a huge month. It was then that I wrote out a much shorter version of the story you are reading now. I wrote it out for a couple different reasons. I wrote it as an attempt to connect to the community. The way I grew up, we shared just about everything. Honesty and openness have been how I have always tried to live my life, with the exception of my *big* secret, and it seemed to work out well for me, for the most part. I also hoped it would help at least one person that was out there like me feel less alone as they realized they had a similar story. Most importantly, I wrote it for myself. I had no idea what all of this meant, and I was determined that writing it all out would in some way help me. I never imagined how much it would begin to change my life.

After I wrote my story, I decided to create a blog to share it with the world in hopes that someone out there would benefit by reading it. I never imagined what my little blog would turn into.

When I started my blog, I only thought I would be sharing my story. It grew to be something remarkable. I turned it into a place where anyone could share their story. My original blog description read:

Crossdressers are commonly misunderstood. This blog is designed primarily for crossdressers, or anyone who wants to learn more about our experiences and why we are the way we are. These are our true stories. If you are a crossdresser with a story, please contact me so I can share your story. ***No nastiness or HATE will be tolerated!

As I evolved through my journey, I realized many of us are very similar, yet different. The majority of people in the world are cisgender. (Unlike many people have come to believe, cis is not a slur. *Cis* means "on this side," so *cisgender* means someone whose gender identity and sex assigned at birth are on the same side.) For many people who are not cisgender, it makes sense to use crossdressing as a means to express themselves or to find themselves. In my thirty-plus years of dressing, I never knew what it meant; then I started searching for the *why* through therapy, research and reflection. I took it all very seriously, working to figure it out and understand the different parts of the community I now called myself part of. After that, I updated the blog description:

Crossdressing is commonly misunderstood. There are a wide variety of reasons one crossdresses: to express oneself, to find oneself, etc. All reasons are valid and sometimes one's reason evolves, as does life. This blog was created for anyone who wants to learn more about our experiences and why we are the way we are. These are our true stories . . .

Thousands read my story and many of them reached out to tell me they were either inspired, or felt connected and less alone, as they had experienced similar things in their life. *This* is what gave me the fire and determination to continue to share and explore deeper. After writing out my story, I came to a *huge* revelation: I fully accepted that there was no way to get this to fade.

For the first time in my life, I realized that *I did not want it to.*

I had tried everything from a lot of prayer, to not dressing, to dressing for forty-two days straight, slowly purging my clothes, etc., and I still had that desire to dress and feel like a woman. When I felt like a woman, I loved every second of it! I realized it was just part of me and I came to peace with that, and now loved that side of me. I thought, *I am still the same me, I just have two sides.*

When I originally wrote my story, I was sure I had no desire to transition. I wrote, "I love being a man, and the man my wife knows and loves. I am still getting to know the other side of me, but I do know that she loves to feel pretty, elegant, classy, and sexy."

https://www.jennspire.com/9-jenn-emerging-sharing

The Why

My wife and I had many conversations over the years. The common thread I recall in all of them was that what bothered her most about my desire to dress was not understanding *why*, and me not being able to answer that question myself. At the time, I was not able to answer that question because I truly did not know the answer. I started to find the answer after I found an online community of people like me. I found myself seeking more and more answers. I talked to people, continued searching the internet, and spent a lot of time reflecting. It was then I noticed a lot of my Facebook friends had liked a Facebook page called "The Fox and the Phoenix Podcast."

I searched "The Fox and the Phoenix Podcast" and it turned out it was a podcast solely about "de-mystifying the crossdressing experience." I listened to one episode and fell in love. Everything about it resonated with me. I decided to go back to Episode 1 and listen to every one in order.

Savannah Hauk, one of the co-hosts, said she was a crossdresser "like me" and I felt a connection which pushed me to want to hear what else she had to say. She explained that she was "dual gender." I immediately thought that was interesting, but that it was definitely *not* me. I remember listening to more and more episodes, and after listening and self-reflection, however, I thought, *That is exactly me. I love my male life with my family, but I also have this female life that I cannot give up without losing part of myself, even if I wanted to.* I continued to listen to the podcast and chat with friends on Facebook, until one day in August 2021 I decided to join Instagram, but we'll get to that later.

Struggles with My Wife

It was obvious from "Little House on the Prairie" day (the time I convinced my girlfriend, who became my wife, to dress me up and put makeup on me and she appeared disgusted the entire night) and every difficult conversation my wife and I had since regarding my dressing, trans people, LGBTQIA+ related topics, etc., that this would be a huge, uphill battle I was about to trek! But this was my *wife*, who was my best friend, whom I never wanted to hide anything from.

The entire time I wrote my story, I so desperately wanted to share it with her, but I knew I needed to figure it out on my own—so that I knew and understood myself enough to be able to share and be fully open with her, explaining who I was and answering all of her questions.

After I figured it all out, or so I thought, I knew I had to share my story with her. One day after the kids went to bed, I pulled out a printed copy of my story and told her I had something I needed to tell her and share with her. Despite a lot of resistance, she finally read it, and told me to leave the room. It was an extremely emotional evening for both of us. We both cried and talked about everything. I explained and shared everything I could think of that was true for me at the time that night. It was one of the toughest nights of my entire life.

I desperately wanted her to accept and love all of me, or at least show a small sign that she could, but that did not happen. Instead, she challenged me to find a way to *fix me* and to give it all up. She wanted me to see a Christian counselor, and she wanted me to have my hormone levels checked. I did not want to do either, but I knew for her I would try, so I did.

One of the things she mentioned was getting an estrogen and testosterone test. I tried a mail-in saliva test that included both T and E. When I got my results, it said my testosterone was normal and my estrogen was a tad high, but it appeared that something else was high, which might be causing the estrogen to read higher. I told my wife, and she appeared eager to try to lower my estrogen.

I tried to explain why my estrogen level was normal and eventually told her I am not going to do anything to try to lower it.

The other thing she mentioned that I agreed to try was counseling. She wanted me to see a Christian counselor, with the idea they might challenge my way of thinking and could be part of this 'fix' my wife appeared to be hopeful for. I struggled to find anyone who claimed to be a Christian counselor that dealt with transgender issues until I found *her*. Counselor #1 was in a nearby city, so I reached out. After a fifteen-minute phone consultation, we really connected. The first time we met, we both agreed that she did not have immense experience with transgender issues, and that if either of us felt I needed more of a gender specialist, we would tell the other. I felt very comfortable with her, and shared my entire story, and all kinds of thoughts I had never shared with anyone else. She and I had met twice, and then the week before my third appointment, I received an email from her that was about to *rock my world*. I will get to that, but I'm trying my best to share all of this in chronological order.

The Lifeline

During several of the conversations I had with my wife, the point I remember that she continued to repeat was about it being an addiction that was controlling me.

On July 25, 2021, after my wife and I had been having our latest of many fights about my crossdressing, I reached out to my friends on Facebook and wrote:

> *Sisters, I need your help . . . my wife is convinced my crossdressing is an addiction and that I just need to fight it. She says because my need to dress once a month so I don't think about it constantly and that I don't have control over it and that I would let something like this come between my family and me are all proof it's an addiction. Please help me explain that it is not.*

I received some great responses, but no response was as powerful as the response I would receive months later. Julie Rubenstein, one of hosts of "The Fox and Phoenix Podcast," reached out and said they would like to use my story, especially my call for help, as the basis of an episode and wanted to know if that would be all right?

"Absolutely," I replied. I was dying to hear the episode! It was released at the beginning of November 2021, and called, "Episode 61 - Angst, Addiction, and Acceptance." In the episode, Julie and Savannah discussed my plea and Julie read her response:

> *IT IS NOT an addiction! If it was, you would not be able to control your crossdressing to once a month. It would be an itch you had to scratch more than once a month; you just couldn't help yourself. Crossdressing is a part of who you are. It is a side of you that must be nurtured. It is not like an addiction. Addiction would mean that you would continue in spite of all the negative consequences, to have lost control and not be able to stop. You crossdress once a month because there is a part of your inside that identifies as female. There is nothing addictive about you and the only negative side effect is your wife's lack of information. Oh honey, you have made the choice to come out to her and you are currently dealing with push back. Whenever you add a level of radical newness to a partnership, there is going to be a push back. It may be a just for now mentality. I love you!*

Savannah pointed out during the discussion that the latest Diagnostic and Statistical Mental Disorders Manual (DSM) in DSM 5 declassified transgender as a disorder, as it is *not* a mental illness. She also reconfirmed that if this was an addiction, I would be doing it every possible moment I could get my hands on it—regardless of it affecting my relationship, job, friendships, family life, etc.

They both continued sharing many more valuable insights in the episode that I recommend that you check out!

Instagram

I had always heard a lot of people talk about Instagram, in both parts of my life. After several people suggested I join, I decided to give it a try. I used the same name, even the same username handle that I had created for Facebook @luvjennifermarie. I started posting pictures, and people were liking them. Since I used my alias, and I was so confident that no one I knew would immediately recognize me, I felt comfortable posting pictures of my face. I did not ever disclose my location nor post pictures in recognizable places, however. I was following all kinds of accounts, and liking their pictures. Soon I started following accounts of beautiful trans women, and women in various parts of the gender spectrum. I had no idea how large the spectrum was, but I soon began to learn.

My Instagram following grew rapidly and while that was fun, what I loved most was all of the new people that my story was reaching and helping. They reached out daily, and it made me smile at the fact that I could help someone just by sharing my story.

I started writing what I called my "black-and-white posts," where I posted a black-and-white picture of me, and shared the deep struggles I was experiencing. That honesty and vulnerability resonated with people, too. It validated what I was feeling when I had no one in person to talk to, and it helped people, so I started doing it routinely. Whenever something came up, I would write it all down, refine it, and share it when I felt the time was right.

Another thing I never expected to happen on Instagram: people were always complimenting me on my looks, and thought I was some sort of expert. It was hard to believe. I never claimed to be any kind of fashion or makeup guru, but I did think it would be fun to start sharing tips as a new way to connect with people. I called this series of posts "Thrifty Girl." Through this series, I shared ways I had found to crossdress without breaking the bank. Some of the topics included thrift store shopping, high heels, wigs, fake nails, and makeup. I had so much fun with these posts that I could see my fun feminine side coming out in more ways than one.

Unclockable

Halloween 2021 was approaching, and I learned I was not the only one thinking about the holiday. One of the transgender women that I followed, had promoted that @UnclockableYou was having a "Hot Girl Halloween Giveaway." All you had to do was like the post and start following both Unclockable and her account. I figured that was easy, so I liked the post, followed both accounts and then continued on with life.

On October 8th, I received a direct message from Unclockable that I had won two free tuck kits. (In case you are wondering, a tuck kit is a specially shaped bandage that is worn "down south" to smooth the equipment of a male-to-female person anatomically.) I had never won anything like this so I thought about how I could do this safely, especially with the sensitive private nature of this product. I gave them my address and received a tracking number shortly. Next, I thought to myself, *I cannot let this arrive at my house!* As I saw it was on the way, I went to the post office to see what I could do. They said I could put a stop-hold on our mail, so I did for a couple days until I saw it had been held at the post office. I retrieved the mail and opened it. There they were, two tuck kits! I was so excited to give it a try!

Within the next two weeks, I had the house to myself for a day, so I eagerly gathered all of my things and the Unclockable tuck kit. I watched the videos of how to use it, and followed the directions the best that I possibly could. It was a *game changer*! I was so smooth for a couple hours I almost forgot I was not a girl *down there*. I had never experienced gender euphoria like that! It was after that experience that I announced on both my Jennifer Marie Facebook and Instagram "I am dual gender/bigender and proud of it!"

Dual Gender and What It Meant to Me

Over the years I had a lot of people ask me, "What is dual gender, and what does it mean for you?" This answer looks different for different people.

Gender Wiki defines it as a term used to describe someone with competing gender traits. Normally someone who is dual gendered has two different gender traits or "people" inside them that will sometimes conflict resulting in dysphoria.

It took me several months to be able to fully explain it. In the end, here is what I went with: *For me, it meant I felt like I was male and female, but when I was in male mode, I did not want to wear anything feminine, and in female mode I wanted to present only as female. Sure, I tried on feminine clothes on a male day, but I never liked it at all. I just wanted to see if they fit, so I was ready the next time I could present how I wanted to.*

I never liked dressing without full makeup. I did not feel complete. As I continued to experience new things, other things made me feel incomplete unless they were part of my presentation. For example, after I experienced Unclockable, I did not even feel like me until I had my Unclockable tuck. As I continued to explore being Jenn, I hated using my male voice. I tried all kinds of ways to alter my voice, but at the time I found that restricting my vocal cords made my pitch a little higher, which made me happy. After all these things were done, I felt like Jenn and felt complete, or at least as complete as I possibly could at that time.

https://www.jennspire.com/10-jenn-emerging-dual-gender

A New Year's Eve I Will Never Forget

New Years Eve 2021 I was at work, and I began having a sharp pain in my side. It started slowly and I thought maybe if I drank water and breathed deeply it would go away. I was in so much pain I decided to lie on the floor underneath my desk, so no one would see me, and everyone would leave me alone. After lying there a little bit, I started sweating and realized I needed to get to the bathroom quickly. I won't share the disgusting details, but afterward, I laid on the floor of the bathroom and called my wife to pick me up. She didn't answer, so I called my mother to come get me. I laid there until she was almost to the office building.

I loaded my things into my mother's car and we went to the hospital for what I expected was pancreatitis. I laid sprawled out in pain in the ER until they called me back. COVID was running rampant, so all of the rooms were taken, but they had a bed in a hallway for me. I was eager to be seen, so I agreed. The nurse asked me some questions and determined that based on some unrelated symptoms that I might have COVID. They asked Mom to leave, and did a couple tests for COVID and kidney stones. It turned out I had both COVID *and* kidney stones. I was sent home to take some medicine, drink lots of liquids, and pass the stone.

I was not a big sugary soda drinker, so that could not have been the cause. I later learned that stress can be a cause of kidney stones. I am determined that all the stress surrounding these incredibly difficult conversations with my wife about who I was, and the stress of our relationship had given me kidney stones.

Beginning to Accept All of Me

The first week of April 2022 I said something that I never thought I would say: "I am done with shame!" I realized that there was absolutely nothing wrong with me, and it felt great to say that.

That did not mean I felt ready to run around telling everyone yet. It meant I was happy with who I was, and I said to myself,

> *I will share my truth with individuals whenever I am ready. If they find out before, then that's fine too. If that changes our relationship, then that's on them. I am super happy with where I am, and I can't wait to see what's in store next!*

https://www.jennspire.com/11-jenn-emerging-beginning-to

Am I Trans Enough?

It's a question that many people in the trans community ask themselves. For me, the first time I asked that question was when someone on Instagram commented on one of my posts asking me to remove trans hashtags, as according to them, "crossdressers are not trans." I responded with a public post that said this:

I want to clarify where I am at. I don't really identify with the term crossdresser anymore, but I keep using it to reach other people like me who are still finding themselves. My main purpose with social media is to help people like me feel less alone. It's the reason I started my blog. I was alone in this for so long (30 years), so I know how it feels. I don't hate the term, and crossdressing is how I express myself as Jenn, but it's not how I personally identify myself anymore.

I identify as dual gender, bigender, genderfluid without the fluid. I don't really like to mix the two sides. My ideal situation would be to be Jenn one full day a week.

So, I would say I am about 85 percent male and 15 percent female.

So, to answer the question . . . I am trans enough for me.

My post stirred up a lot of conversation on social media, so much that "The Fox and Phoenix Podcast" reached out, again, and talked about it during a good portion of episode 83 titled "Trans Enough." I'm not going to summarize the episode, but I recommend checking it out.

There is a lot of gatekeeping within the LGBTQIA+ community. You may not know what I mean by *gatekeeping*, so let me try to explain from my perspective. Inside the community, gatekeeping can look like people who tell you that you have to be this certain way, and experience certain things, to designate yourself as such. Many people outside the LGBTQIA+ community are trying to put us in boxes, but the ridiculous thing is it happens inside as well! Luckily, it appears to be getting better.

For example, I am sure there are some transgender individuals (I will not say how many) that think I am not transgender, because I did not feel tortured and lived a mostly happy life before transition. I have even had bisexual friends who have been told they are not part of the community, because they are in heteronormative man and woman relationships. I am completely against any gatekeeping.

For anyone reading this: However you feel is who you are and *don't you dare* let anyone else convince you otherwise.

The surprising thing about my post was that the transgender woman who made that comment about me not being transgender later sent me a really nice message after my post and apologized. She told me she was sorry, she understood, and that she would like to be friends.

Chapter Five

Jenn Rising

As I explained previously, April 14, 2021, was the day I created my name and joined social media. I never knew how significant that was until the following year.

My real birthday is in March, and in 2022 I did not seem to care about it as much as I typically do. I spent it getting excited for my Jenn birthday the next month.

On April 15, 2022, I posted: *Thank you for the birthday wishes yesterday! It really meant a lot! Nobody here knew it was Jenn's birthday yesterday . . . one of the many things I am trying to figure out if I am okay with . . .*

It was really difficult, because I knew these feelings meant something.

https://www.jennspire.com/12-jenn-rising

A Local Friend Like Me

A couple months after I joined Instagram, I reached out to a younger person who lives near me, who was very public about the fact that they identified as a crossdresser. They went by Jess. Jess was so open about it; I read an article online about how he even put it on his dating profile.

I was going through so much discovery that I needed to talk to someone about this, and I love speaking in person. I felt Jess was a safe person, so I sent him the following message:

> *I am kind of scared even writing this, because you are the first person beside my wife whom I have ever told I crossdress and that I live in the area. I don't know if you know any other crossdressers in the area, but I don't. I would love to meet you for coffee in guy mode sometime, just to connect, as I know you are someone who is a lot like me. Are you open to that?*

Jess quickly responded and made my day. He was open to meeting, and willing to meet however I felt most comfortable. We had lunch at a local LGBTQIA+ friendly restaurant in guy mode, and instantly connected. It was so helpful having someone I could talk to about this in person and so freely.

We continued to meet for lunch about once a month for the next year and a half. Everytime we met, we each had things we wanted to share. It was so therapeutic! He encouraged me by explaining that counseling really helped him, and that I should give it a try. I told him I was planning to.

"I need to get out in the world as Jenn," I told him during one of our lunches. "Any chance we could meet up someday at your place, dress up, and head out? If it's weird, just let me know. I will totally understand."

"That sounds great!" he exclaimed, and seemed super-excited about it. We put a date on the calendar—and I was counting down the days!

First Day Out

To prepare for Jenn's first time out, I started to acquire clothing and accessories that were not only cute, but would allow me to blend in when I was ready. I bought my first pair of women's pants. They were skinny jeans. I also bought a cute, long-sleeve top and accessories on Amazon. One of our other crossdressing friends from Instagram was coming in for the week, so it worked perfectly for him to join us.

I had taken off work for the day so after everyone was gone, I packed my car and headed to Jess's apartment. When I arrived, I hauled my suitcases and bags in, and laid out everything I wanted to wear. After over an hour and a half, I was ready. Jess was still getting ready, so the three of us chatted and got to know each other while he finished. I loved how similar, yet different, all three of us were.

We left the apartment to go to a restaurant nearby for lunch. As I walked out of the building, I could feel the anticipation building and my heart pounding. (*Here we go Jenn . . . it's all or nothing!*) As I walked to the car, I caught a couple glances from people, but nothing more than a look. We then drove to the restaurant.

As I stepped out of the car I knew *this is it* . . . I could see cars and people, and I knew they were about to see me. I knew I would be noticed, as I am 6' 2", but I stepped one foot after the other as femininely and gracefully as I could in my three-inch black heels. People looked at us, but no more than I looked at someone when they passed me.

All the staff and guests were very friendly! Yes, even though they were friendly, I could not get outside of my own head. It took me a while to settle into being Jenn, and I'm not sure I ever fully did that day. Looking back on it, when I was at home in my space with my lighting taking selfies, it was all in my control and being able to see my facial reactions gave me immense joy . . . but now none of it was in my control, and there were people everywhere. It was overwhelming! Everything was so new it was so difficult to calm down and fully embrace being Jenn.

We had a great lunch and conversation, and then it was back to the car to drive to an event space to meet the photographer for our photo shoot, Jenn's *first* ever professional shoot!

We pulled up to the building, got our bags out of the trunk, and walked to the front door where we were greeted by the photographer. She greeted us with a cheerful, "Hi, ladies!"

That was the first time I was ever greeted by someone as a *lady*, and it felt great!

We walked up a couple flights of stairs in this rustic building to a gorgeous event space, and took in the beauty of it while we hung up our outfits. After a little makeup touch-up, I was ready for the fun to begin.

We each took all kinds of photos and had a good time. I was not in love with my makeup, so it took me a while to fall into being Jenn. I felt more like Jenn after I attached my fake nails. After I had settled into being Jenn, we took some group pics, and it was time to pack up.

On the way back to Jess's place, we reveled in the activities of the day. We each talked about everyday life and plans for the future. Then we all hugged and went our separate ways.

I am sure I could have slowly gone out in public myself, but having my friends by my side, with their experience presenting in public, made me so much more at ease. I am still so grateful for them!

https://www.jennspire.com/13-jenn-rising-first-day-out

Counseling, Part I

As I shared with you before, I felt very comfortable with Counselor #1, so much so that I shared my entire story and all kinds of personal thoughts I had never shared with anyone else. She and I had met twice and then the week before my third appointment I received an email from her.

My counselor explained she had some personal things going on and was stepping away from counseling. I remember wanting to cry and being mad. I was mad that she let me start counseling with her, only to leave me after two sessions.

I was not a runner and it was midnight, but I decided I needed to go for a run, something I hadn't done for a long time. There were times on that run that I sprinted, and others that I just broke down and cried while I walked. I made it back home a calmer version of myself than before.

Then I re-read the email:

> *I'm reaching out to let you know that I've made some changes in my life and am stepping away from my practice as a counselor. It hasn't been an easy decision. I'm not going anywhere else at this time. If I were, I would tell you for sure.*
>
> *This is just a crappy email for me to write to you (crappy is not a clinical word, obviously) because we just started working together. I know you are benefiting from a safe space to share your thoughts. If you would be open to seeing another counselor, we have two here*

*that could be a match. But also, I know opening up and building
another relationship can be hard. I know what it took for you to
reach out to me.*

*I'm still planning on us meeting on Tuesday to process this and other
things further. But reach out if you have questions or thoughts.*

I decided to go to our final session to share the things I had written
down, wrap things up, hear who she thought would be good for me
to see, and say goodbye.

I was in a very good head space when I arrived at our final session.
I went through my list of things I wanted to talk about and when it
came toward the end, when I planned to hear her list of people she
recommended for me, I felt a great calm come over me. Instead of
asking to hear her list, I proceeded to explain that I thought I would
be frustrated and not want my sessions with her to end, but I felt
like I was in a much better place.

"Do you think I am in the right place where it would be beneficial
for me to see a gender therapist[4]?" I asked her. She explained that
she was so happy with my progress, and could see how much more
comfortable with myself I had become; she also thought I could
really benefit from seeing a gender therapist. I decided right then
that's exactly what I would do.

---

4. "The primary role of a gender therapist is to provide support, guidance, and counseling
to individuals as they navigate their gender identity journey. They create a safe and non-
judgmental space where clients can explore their feelings, thoughts, and experiences
related to gender."
Charlie Health, "What Is a Gender Therapist?," accessed July 11, 2024, https://www.
charliehealth.com/post/what-is-a-gender-therapist#:~:text=The%20primary%20role%20
of%20a,and%20experiences%20related%20to%20gender.

I reached out to the gender therapist I had come across several times over the years of searching online and scheduled a session. While reaching out, I recalled this was the same counselor I had emailed seven years prior. At that time, I was too scared to take it any further, but now I knew it was the right time and place to figure me out, no matter what that meant.

I saw Counselor #2 a few times. Instead of me telling her my entire story, she told me to write it down. I told her I had already done that. She said I want you to think about being transgender as you write your story again. This version is going to be through a transgender lens. I was not too excited to do it all again, but I knew I needed to.

As I did all this soul searching, I realized when I wrote that original version, I wrote it from the lens of a crossdresser. I never considered I was transgender. When I wrote it through a trans lens, my story grew exponentially. I recalled so many more pieces of the story I am sharing with you, many of them much deeper than my original story.

Counselor #2 also asked me to meditate, something I had never done. She told me to close my eyes, to just be still and listen to myself thinking about the following questions:

- *How would you feel if your body were to change?* As I did this, I began to be happy at the thought of having a more feminine figure, longer hair, smooth skin, etc.
- *How did you feel about lying to your mother when she asked in college how you were doing with all of this? What would your*

father do if he knew about you? As I thought about this, I knew it killed me keeping this from my mother. It always had. Whenever I was around her, I wanted to tell her so badly, as we were always so close. As I thought about my father, I knew he would be shocked and not know how to deal with it, at least for a while, but I knew he loved me deeply and he would still love me after. I finally realized the reason I did not want my father to know: I did not think he would understand, and I did not want his view of me to change. I was his fishing, sports, beer drinking buddy and I did not want any of that to go away.

- *You say you are dual gender, but do you love your male body or just the male privilege that comes with it?* I had to meditate about this for a while and in the end, I realized I never loved my male body. I was never settled in it. What I loved was how I was treated and how many things came easy for me. I also realized that I was always trying to reinvent my hair, getting at least one new style every year or so. I was never happy with my hair. As I continued to sit in silence, I realized I wanted it to be long and feminine.

I made a lot of progress and learned a lot about myself with Counselor #2, but she was always telling me, "You are trans." I was starting to wonder about this more and more, but I needed to figure it out myself, so I moved on to find the type of counselor I needed.

I met with Counselor #3 twice. We only met twice because all she did was listen. I needed someone who was not just a listener, but would ask me questions and provide insight.

Then I found her! Counselor #4 was amazing, and I knew it even after our first session. She asked great questions and every session I left with some insight.

It felt safe to tell her anything, so I shared my innermost thoughts. Here are just a few of my thoughts or conversations we had over the year that I met with her:

> "I feel like I am one step closer to something big. I don't know what that is yet, but it feels big!"

> "I feel like I am boxed in. I know I put myself in that box and didn't consider anything else . . ." Her response was, "There is no right way to be trans—you don't have to grow up hating your body."

> "I know being Jenn full-time would blow up my family . . ." She replied "Choosing Jenn is a wound being healed, not an act of abandonment of family."

> "I struggle to consistently think of myself as Jenn." She said, "It's easier to think of yourself as (him). It is a defense mechanism that is trying to keep you *safe*."

The First Letter

You may be wondering after moving into the house, doing renovations on the house, and all of the work on myself, what has happened with my marriage and my kids. Well, it was about this time that I was finally confident in who I was that it was time for my wife and I to have another conversation.

I was still so in love with my wife that even after that excruciating and heartbreaking night of me sharing everything and receiving nothing in return, except her not leaving me, I refused to give up on us. As weeks and months went on, I realized I had more to share, so I wrote a letter and shared it with her:

Love of my life,

First off, I love you so much. I appreciate you sticking by me through everything.

I want to tell you about my counseling . . . I started with a Christian counselor. It was very difficult to find someone that listed Christian on their Psychologytoday.com profile. She was amazing and I loved every one of my three sessions with her. She had never worked with someone quite like me, but she listened and challenged me to open up. She made it easy to open up to her. She was so respectful of my privacy, so much that she never really wrote down anything concrete in case someone was to read it, because of my public presence in the community. At the end of the first session, she told me two things . . . first she said, "You light up when you talk about (insert my girl name)" and she said "The other thing you light up about is when you talk about your wife." I already knew both were extremely important but that was amazing to hear.

As you know before our third session, I was a wreck after I read that she was leaving counseling. My midnight run helped a bit. I came back and re-read the email and it said our last session would be next week and she was looking forward to seeing me then. I decided to go to our final session to share the things I had written down, wrap things up, hear who she thought would be good for me to see, and say goodbye.

I was in a very good headspace when I arrived at our final session. I went through my list of things I wanted to talk about and when it came toward the end when I planned to hear her list of people she recommended for me, I felt a great calm come over me. Instead of asking to hear her list, I proceeded to explain that I thought I would be frustrated and not want my sessions with her to end, but I felt like I was in a good place. I asked her if I could ask her a question. I asked her, "Do you think I am in the right place where it would be beneficial for me to see a gender therapist?" She explained that she was so happy with my progress and could see how much more comfortable with myself I had become. She also said she thought I could really benefit from seeing a gender therapist as they know a lot more about gender identity than she did. The last thing she told me was that she knew that you struggled with this side of me, but it was important that I tell you one thing . . . she asked me if I remembered the first thing I said to her in our first session. I did not remember. She said, "You told me I want to make this work with my wife. I'm crazy about her!"

I reached out to the gender therapist I had come across several times over the years of searching online and we scheduled a session. I remembered I had emailed this same person back in 2015, but after she responded, I was too scared to take it any further. I felt like I was now in the right place and time to figure me out.

The therapist I am currently seeing has been doing this for over twenty years. I have made some good progress with her. I realized I can't continue to live in this current state. Taking a day off work here and there to dress up

. . . I need to have my space and time because I know you don't understand it but the girl in me is real. I need to be out in the world, like any other girl. What does that look like? I would like to go out, sometimes on trips. I have friends here that I would like to go out with. I also have friends that want me to come see them and I think those are great opportunities to go out.

I am not saying you have to meet my female side right now because I know you are not interested. I also know you said you are worried that if you see me, it will ruin how you view me. I am worried that you not wanting anything to do with that side of me will cause us to grow further and further apart. I am wanting us to be closer and to share all of me with you, if you let me. I have kept it secret for so long, mostly because I didn't understand it, but you are my person and I'm wanting to share my world with you, so we can continue to walk through life together, instead of letting it drive us apart.

The other thing that really hurts is when you talk negatively about LGBTQIA+ because I am part of the community and proud of who I am.

Lately, I have been having trouble in bed and trouble with desire to have sex. You keep asking am I not attracted to you anymore. That has absolutely nothing to do with it. My issue that is affecting all of that is that we are both on two different wavelengths. You not agreeing with my community is equating to me that you don't agree with who I am, and it is getting so difficult to put on a happy face. Hence why you keep asking me if I am ok or why I am breathing hard. I need you to show me that you want to be open to understanding who I truly am and love all of me.

Before you quit your job, I asked you if you were here for the long haul and you said yes. I know that after that happened, I changed the game, so I want to ask you again. If you do not want to be here, it will break my heart, but I will do everything to support you and try to give you time to find a career that you want. I love you so much!

As soon as she was done reading that letter, we had one of our most difficult conversations. The only thing I remember was her explaining that I was giving up on her and the kids because she felt I was choosing this over all of them. I tried to explain as best as I could that it had nothing to do with her or the kids and that it was just about me, but I never felt like I could get that through to her. I only hoped over time and continued conversations that she would begin to understand me.

Difficult Journal Entries

I want to do something I have not done in telling you my story, yet. I want to share with you my personal journal entries from the days that followed. I think it will show you the challenges that we both faced and how even after that letter, neither of us were ready to give up on *us*.

Friday

Telling my wife Friday that I'm dual gender, that I need to be public and most of all that I need her to try to love all of me was probably the hardest thing I have done.

I had planned to read the letter I wrote to her after we put the kids to bed. It was obvious as this needed to come because she made comments about me not being attracted to her, so I finally said let's just talk after they go to bed, which made her upset. Then when they went to bed, I got out the letter which made her more upset. She almost didn't let me read it. Then I read it and she experienced just about every emotion.

After I read my wife the letter, we had a lot of difficult conversations. . . She believes I should put her above everything including this. I am not sure how to put her above my true identity.

One of the things we agreed on was that I won't go out in public until we have a discussion, probably in 30 days. During that time, we will go to church and work through things. I also told her it's been so long since my last time and I need a girl day. She agreed.

Saturday

Saturday was equally difficult. . . She told me what I'm doing is a sin and that she is praying for a miracle. I told her, "I'm praying for the same thing," She knew what I meant and got mad.

She also told me that I'm selfish and putting myself above her and the kids which is absolutely untrue.

She also said I should go on testosterone. I refused that one! I have been tested and all my levels are fairly average.

She also would still like me to talk to a new counselor that would challenge me to give it all up. (I did not understand it at the time, but later learned this is conversion therapy which is illegal for licensed counselors to *implement.) I would like her to talk to a gender therapist. Maybe one day I'll agree to see hers if she agrees to see mine.*

She wants me to take a break from social media while we work on us. I explained that I can't, because that's my support system. I think she needs to meet Jenn. I think it would help her understand who I am better. Maybe one day I'll agree if she will.

Sunday

Sunday was a much better day. First, we went to church for the first time since COVID. It was amazing! I left the service feeling closer to God and confirmed I am on the right path. I later told my wife that. Of course, she did not like it, but it's how I truly feel.

A little later she came to me and asked if we both could stop the one-lined zingers attacking the other. We both agreed, and had a much better day focusing on each other and having fun with the kids.

We left the weekend with still a lot to work through but definitely hope and love . . . we are both invested in this marriage, and have hope that we can make it work.

Coming Out to a Few

After I admitted to myself that Jenn was a part of me, and that my marriage might not survive, I knew I needed my support system, so I decided to tell a few key people.

Sister

First, I told my sister. I met her in a park. I had it all written down what I was going to say and as I read her that I currently identify as dual gender and trans questioning, she was so unbelievably supportive that I honestly couldn't think of a way it could have gone better! She said, "I'm not surprised considering our childhood and how much you loved to dress."

I had no idea that she was so trans supportive (and still is). Here were just a few things that came up during our conversation:

- She vividly remembers calling me "Jennifer" when we were growing up, and loves that I used the name.
- She asked to see pictures, so I showed her, and she said I looked great.
- She has so many more LGBTQIA+ friends than I knew about.
- She is a nurse and has even injected one of her friend's kids with hormone-blockers.
- She knows so many great doctors that do facial feminization if I go down that road.
- Most importantly, she told me that she loves me, and nothing could ever change that.
- And lastly, she said she will be here right by my side while I figure it all out.

We hadn't been very close for a while, but this brought us closer than ever.

Parents (Mom and Dad)

As I was writing this book, Mom shared with me that many years ago, their friends' sons came out as gay. That was the first time my parents were prompted to think about how they would react if either I or my sister came out to them. She said that after thinking it over, they knew if one of us told them we were gay, they would not disown us, but continue to love us. We were each their children God had given to them to love. Little my mother knew, this conversation she and my father had would prepare them for my big secret I would share years later.

This also explains why, when I was in middle school, they told me, "Even if you told us you are gay, we are always going to love you!" To this day, that has always made me feel great.

Nonetheless, I was nervous to tell my parents. Even though I knew they would accept me, telling your parents is still a big thing, so I did what I always do when I am doing something monumental: I reflect, analyze, research, plan, and execute.

My sister and I decided to have my parents come over to her house during my lunch hour one day. I told her that she needed to tell them that they could not tell anyone what they were doing that day, because they were not going to be able to tell anyone what I was going to share. It turns out, my parents thought I was going to tell them I was gay. They learned it was much more than that.

I knew I was going to be nervous and had so much to say, so I wrote it all out. I held my sister's hand tightly as I read the following letter to my parents, as I cried:

If I could tell you my biggest secret that could bring us closer together than ever, but you absolutely couldn't tell anyone, would you want to know?

You won't be able to tell anyone, even family and friends. If this gets out, I could potentially lose my job and my life. You are the second and third people I'm telling, and it's because I love you and trust you and want us to have a great relationship.

I'm under the transgender umbrella. I currently identify as trans questioning. I'm currently seeing a gender therapist to figure out exactly where I fit.

I was born this way, and I believe God made me this way for a reason. I know, because I get to help people every day by inspiring them on social media. I know, because they reach out to me on almost a daily basis.

Ever since I was four years old, I have spent just about every possible minute dressing up as a woman. I have used dress up play time, Halloween, spirit days, convinced women into dressing me up including mom, my sister, and many others. I always thought it was about dressing up, but as I have gotten older and also sought therapy, I realized it's a lot more.

My first day of therapy with a general therapist at the end of my first session she said, "You light up when you talk about 'her name,' and when you talk about your wife." I realized even more how important both women are. And yes "she" has a name. When you are ready to hear it, I will tell you what it is and why.

More than anything, I want you both to know that while I was born this way, I do know that I don't regret not knowing sooner because you gave me a wonderful childhood that I loved. I also wouldn't have my beautiful, amazing children. So, for those reasons, I do not regret any of it.

I hope no matter what happens that we can still have a great relationship. Mom, I hope we can grow closer and Dad, I hope we can, too. Dad, even if I change, I still hope we can be craft beer-drinking fishing buddies.

I don't expect you to know what to say right away, but know I love you and know you can ask me absolutely anything anytime.

Throughout the entire 90-minute conversation, they were extremely loving, calm, and asked great questions. I couldn't have asked for a better conversation.

Mom did most of the talking. She said, "I can't say that I'm that surprised." She also mentioned that I used to love wearing her nightgown, too. I had forgotten that!

Mom could see my pain. It hurt *her* to know I had been hurting over all of those years, not knowing who I really was. I told her I do not regret not knowing, because I would not have the great childhood I had, and I wouldn't have my children.

Dad did not say a whole lot. He did, however, reassure me that he loved me no matter what and it would take him some time, but that they were going to put in the work to be able to best support me.

As the conversation concluded, there were still a lot of things for us to discuss. (And yes, my parents did invite me over several times to talk about all of the challenges for myself and my family, and the possible things I would be giving up.) It was a while until I shared my new name, showed them pictures of me as Jenn, and before they were ready to meet Jenn, but this letter was perfect for one day and left us a lot of room for growth in the future.

My First Friend

Next, I came out to my first friend, Sam. It had been years since I had spoken with Sam, but I chose him because he is gay, and thought he could better relate, would be supportive, but could also keep it to himself. He is also an attorney, and I knew I would need his advice if my marriage ever moved toward divorce. Sam was immediately supportive and continues to send me sweet encouraging messages occasionally. He also told me that whenever I am ready, he would love for Jenn to come visit him for the weekend.

Integration

As I was going through this difficult journey, trying to find my footing and trying to finally be happy and settled inside, I did a lot of research, talked to a number of people throughout the gender spectrum and met with four counselors. There was one key recurring theme: *integration.*

When I was speaking with my friends who had found peace and made it work with their spouses, if they were happy, they had integrated. They were either free to express their feminine nature when they needed or wanted to, or they found happiness in between both genders, typically by underdressing.

What is underdressing?

Underdressing is a term that is used for the act of wearing women's undergarments under one's male clothes while they are in male mode. This can be done with panties, a bra, pantyhose, corset, etc.

Most people just wear panties and maybe a bra, but there are more adventurous people who wear more than that. There are people who do it for the rush, but I have found mostly it is done to connect with one's feminine self.

But this is where I never fit the box. I knew I never fit and probably never would. I couldn't fit into this dual gender box for one big reason . . . I was just scared to admit it to myself. I hated the "in-between."

I tried wearing panties and a bra under my male clothes, like many of my friends who identified as gender-fluid or dual gender were doing. It gave them connection to their feminine selves, but every time I did it, I felt uncomfortable in so many ways. When I told people I was dual gender, I would sometimes add, "gender-fluid without the fluid." I learned there is no such thing as gender-fluid *without* being fluid.

Most of the people who find happiness without transitioning like the fluid aspect. As hard as I tried, I could not do it. I wanted to present as all him or all her, but really, I just wanted to be *all her*.

You would have been able to see this even in the way I talked about myself with people that knew about Jenn. When I would talk about myself, I would refer to each side in the third person. I would say, "my Jenn side . . ."

I vividly remember my Counselor #2 telling me, "Stop objectifying yourself. Stop talking about Jenn in the third person . . . you are Jenn! You need to think about the two identities coming together and merging." I could not connect the two, even when I was just talking about myself; how *could* I merge?

I would integrate and find that happy place within, but that would come later and would be done in a way I never imagined in my wildest dreams.

Is Being Jenn a Sexual Thing?

Here is an excerpt from my journal that I wrote back on July 17, 2022:

Is being Jenn sexual? I will never deny that at one point in my life I thought it was. My heart was pounding, and I was experiencing sheer joy . . . I don't need to go into it, but it never really was the same.

Yesterday, I was having a great conversation with one of my best friends from Instagram. She made the best point that makes total sense, at least for me. Back when I was learning about my sexuality, I had no idea what gender euphoria was, so maybe I confused it with sexuality. Both are a kind of an adrenaline rush. So, if I could go back in time and tell my younger self something, I would say, "Do not confuse gender euphoria with sexual excitement."

The Second Letter

After the first letter, my wife and I continued to have difficult conversations many nights after the kids had gone to bed. After weeks had passed, I experienced another revelation and knew I needed to share it with her, so I wrote her a second letter. This time I insisted that I read it to her, and she allowed it.

I need to tell you something for multiple reasons:

> *I love you and I want us to have absolute honesty, because I think that's our only chance of moving forward.*

> *To show you I really am trying to put you first while still being true to myself.*

> *My body is literally screaming at me to tell you.*

When I told you how I identified, that was true—but only partially true. I identify as dual gender, trans-questioning. I have been questioning for a while now. I question whether I have to transition to be happy.

I tell you this not to scare you, but out of those reasons I mentioned and show you how invested I am in this relationship that I'm trying to make this work and find a way for us both to be happy.

I am proposing we each see whatever counselors we want to, but we also see a mutual counselor together to find something that works for both of us.

Also, I wonder if part of the reason I am questioning is that I have no girl time so my brain gets going and thinking . . . if I was her all the time, I wouldn't have to find time to express my feminine side and I wouldn't have to juggle the two lives. When can I have a full day at home by myself, or would it be easier if I just did it at a friend's right now?

The night I shared that letter with her was another difficult night. She was not interested in talking much that night, so I just let it be.

Chapter Six

Trying to Have it All

Three days after I gave my wife that second letter, I noticed I had a rash on my stomach. I assumed it was poison ivy, as I had been working outside with my shirt off and for the last several years I had gotten poison ivy just about every year. I applied some of my poison ivy cream to it, and it did not get better. In fact, it got really painful. I showed it to my sister, who is a nurse, and she said I needed to have a doctor look at it.

When I walked into urgent care, the nurse practitioner immediately looked at the rash and said, "That is shingles. Have you been under stress? Because that is likely the cause." I told her, "Yes." and left it at that.

She prescribed me some medicine and within a few days, it started to improve a little bit, but it took a month to get a lot better. I did not dare tell anyone in my personal life that I was in pain and that I had shingles, because at my age, the cause could only be stress. I could not tell anyone *why* I was stressed, and that was the worst part; I didn't want them asking questions that might lead them to the truth. So, I just kept quiet and smiled.

It started to make me angry that *I* knew who *I* was, but the conflict that I was having with my wife was affecting my health. I voiced this frustration to my wife, but it just turned into another fight.

"Things I Know"

Shortly after I shared that difficult second letter with my wife, I knew I still wasn't ready to give up on her. I wanted her to feel special, because she was so special to me! I wrote her a small note:

Things I Know

I LOVE YOU.
You are beautiful in every way.
I have learned to appreciate your natural beauty more than ever.
I love being your teammate.
You are a great Mother.
I want you to be my best friend again.
I will ALWAYS love you no matter what.
I want to see a counselor with you that we both can agree on.

The Response

For weeks after the second letter, we did not talk much. When she was ready to talk, it felt like she had a lot to say. Those moments were a bit of a blur, but I remember the words that hit hardest for me were these:

- She still wanted the best for me, whether I believed that or not.
- She didn't feel safe around me anymore, because I was the one in control of the future, which I could understand.
- She had feelings of uncertainty which made her not even want to buy anything for the house anymore.
- She didn't want me to touch her anymore, which was why she had been sleeping on the couch almost every night.
- To her, it felt like an ongoing affair, a common feeling that I have heard that other spouses in similar situations have experienced.
- I was not the same guy she married because my views had changed. I explained that I had grown and evolved (which is what I believe people are supposed to do.)
- Every normal thing we used to do seemed fake if we did it now. For example, planning a party, holding hands, etc.
- She didn't want the kids to go to bed because she was afraid I would tell her something else.
- She *finally* agreed that we both needed to each see a counselor. She insisted that I see a counselor who would dive deep into my past and challenge me, because she believed I had a childhood trauma that I did not remember.
- She asked me if she found someone who had been struggling with their gender identity, but worked through it, would I be willing to talk to them? I was sure I knew Jenn was part of me but I agreed I would be open to a conversation.
- Divorce can mess up kids—I explained that I wanted this to work, and that I was still there because I wanted it to

work. I elaborated and said I had thought many times in some ways it would be easier if we weren't together, but I explained that I loved her and was committed to making this work.

- She would never be okay if she learned my femme name.

- She brought up the time that my counselor said, *"You light up when you talk about [insert my girl name]"* and *"The other thing you light up about is when you talk about your wife."* She could not stop thinking about that. She explained that it feels like "she" is the other woman. – The counselor's comment, a comment I thought would make her happy, instead ended up hurting her.

- She felt like there was more, but she didn't feel like she could take any more.

These were raw conversations with a lot of uncertainty about where we were headed. Ultimately, she was not ready to give up on her husband and her family, and neither was I. We had no idea what our future would look like, but we both wanted to find a way to stay together more than anything!

The Hotel

It was August 2022, and months had gone by without me being able to have time to fully express myself with hair and makeup.

"I haven't been able to express my other self for several months (the last time was April) so I need to have time to myself," I told my wife one day. "Do you want to leave with the kids and give me the house for a day, or do I need to get a hotel?"

I remember her replying calmly as she asked that I go somewhere else because home is her safe place and she did not want things that make her feel unsafe happening there.

A few days later, I told her the date I had booked a hotel for, and it was planned.

The day was here. I told her I was leaving, and that I would be back late the next morning. I heard her sigh as I was leaving the house for the hotel. But I was off!

I had never been out of the house as Jenn before except Halloween, and the time I dressed in Jess's apartment and went out with him. I was excited and nervous. Since this was Jenn's first time out of the house on her own, I never left the hotel. This cute boutique hotel was an old house that was converted into separate rooms. My adventure was leaving my room and taking pictures all over the common areas. I tried on about ten dresses and took hundreds of pictures! It was so much fun! It was quiet in the house, as there were only a few rooms. I only ran into people twice.

The first time I saw two ladies as I was walking upstairs. I squeaked out a "Hi," and put my head down and walked up the stairs to my room.

The second time was at the end of my night. I was taking pictures outside my door. I heard a lady that I had said, "Hello" to earlier in the day in guy mode talking to the ladies downstairs. I could hear her coming up the stairs. I decided I was not going to run back into my room and instead I would keep taking pictures. When she arrived at the top of the stairs, we both smiled at each other and said hello. As small of a gesture as that was, it gave me an amazing feeling!

When I returned home the next day, I was greeted with a warm welcome by my wife. I called it a win.

https://www.jennspire.com/14-the-hotel

Can I Go?

Before I had booked the local hotel, I had been invited to go on a girls' weekend trip with some of my friends that I met through Instagram. I was so nervous to mention this to my wife, but I got up the nerve and told her I was invited, and this was something I needed to do. She told me that it was something she really did not like, and she could not stop me. I booked the flight that night.

The next day, she indicated she really did not want me to go and thought that we should really focus on each other. I told her I had booked it, and I was not going to cancel the trip because I needed to experience this.

We didn't talk about it again until I was packing to leave. She had a ton of questions.

First, she asked where I was going.

"Atlanta," I replied.

She wanted to know what I would be doing there.

"Eating out, shopping, a club, I don't know," I replied.

She appeared to be thinking it over, then asked when I was dressed, if I still felt like I was married to her. At first I didn't understand what she was asking, but then I realized she was wondering if I remained faithful to her.

"Absolutely!" I exclaimed, without hesitation. "I always wear a wedding ring because I am that devoted to you."

Then the conversation shifted to my dressing sessions at home. She asked what I did during those days?

"Dress up, take pics, have lunch, clean, normal stuff," I replied.

She wondered what I did with these pictures.

I said, "I post them online."

She paused again, then continued. She asked if it was sexual for me. I assume she was thinking that if I wasn't having sex outside the marriage, what *was* I doing? What *was* this about? It appeared to me she always wanted to find a way to bring it back to being sexual, to prove her theory that it was a sexual addiction—I assume because an addiction is something that you can fight.

Now it was my turn to pause, then continue. "When I first started as a kid, it obviously wasn't sexual. Then in my teens, I started 'taking care of business' on my own, during or after I dressed, because it became sexual for me. Since I discovered myself, I do it before to become *her* more."

She asked that if it wasn't sexual when I was a kid, what was it?

I told her it took me a long time to figure it out, but it was gender euphoria.

She asked about gender euphoria and what it meant for me.

"Gender euphoria to me is happiness, happiness with myself being myself in my presentation," I responded.

I remember the conversation ending with her stating that she felt like I was choosing this over my family. To illustrate her point, she talked about how it took time and energy away from her and the kids. She stated that I was even choosing to go on trips without them.

My heart went out to her, but I was not about to cancel this trip. "I have always told you I wanted you to be part of my world, this world I'm discovering," I explained. "I want you there."

And then we left it at that for the day.

The next day I was feeling some big emotions, so I needed to put them down. Here's the note that I wrote to my wife that I ended up just keeping to myself in my journal:

I feel like I am standing on the edge of a cliff . . . I am up to the edge. I am really trying not to jump. Every step you take to pull me away is pushing me toward the cliff. It is like when you pull someone's arm to something they do not want to do, they pull away and fall forward. I need to be me, and find balance so I can be stable enough to not jump or fall.

Preparing for the Trip

The entire week before I left, I was nervous but also excited. I was having these feelings for multiple reasons. I had a little bit of nerves because I had barely been out in public, but most of my nerves were about how big this trip would be for me as Jenn. I had been experiencing a lot of dysphoria since my last Jenn day a couple weeks prior. I thought I had figured out my plan . . . get out and dress once a month, and that will make just about everything better. It appeared it did not. I kept thinking, *I do not know if Jenn is going to want to go away after her first full weekend.* I wondered if I would realize Jenn is the true me, and feel I had changes to make in my life for her. It was a lot of feelings all at once, but I knew Jenn was ready to experience life and find out. Before I left, there were a couple of things I wanted to do.

Victoria's Secret

In recent weeks before the trip, I was using a cinch bra I found on Amazon. While it did fine, I was always thinking, *How could I do this better?* Several friends had mentioned the great results they achieved using a Victoria's Secret Bombshell Bra. Okay, if I am going to spend fifty dollars on a bra, I need the right fit! Since I had never been fitted for a bra, I decided to go into the store and ask for help.

During my lunch hour, I walked into Victoria's Secret and pulled one of the employees aside. I'd typed a message I had written on my phone that said, "Is this a trans-friendly store?"

"Absolutely!" she replied.

I showed her one of my best pictures and said, "This is also me. I have never been fitted for a bra. Would you be able to help me with that?" Standing there in my business-casual male mode, showing her these photos, I braced myself for any response . . . because I had no idea what her response might be.

Without batting an eye, she asked me if I would feel more comfortable in the dressing room to get measured. I nodded, relieved.

After the employee measured me in the dressing room, she went out and picked out a Bombshell Bra in my size and brought it to my dressing room. After I had it on, I had her come back and look to make sure that it was the right fit. She thought it was, so I bought it. What a great experience!!

This is exactly how it should be! I thought to myself as I exited the store. Victoria's Secret made a customer for life that day. I could not wait to use my Bombshell on the trip!

Sephora

After I purchased a bra in-store, I was building my confidence, so I was ready to clear another hurdle.

The biggest thing I battled was hiding my five-o'clock shadow. When I presented as Jenn, sometimes the stubble was difficult to look past, so I decided the next step I would take is to walk into Sephora in guy mode to get some help to cover it up.

I showed them a short reel and said this is also me, and asked what they recommended to better cover my facial hair. As I expected, I was treated with respect. She took me right to the color corrector, and showed me an orange shade she thought would be best. She also invited me to try some on. I was not that brave, but I bought some. It was little more than I liked to spend, but since Jenn was venturing out into public for the first time, I figured she was worth the splurge.

First Pedicure

The final thing I wanted to do before I left was to get my first pedicure. I knew I could just wear shoes, or socks until I left to hide my toes, and if my wife or kids did see them, I would just deal with it then.

I walked into the nail salon with my mask on to feel safe and not reveal my face. I was led to the pedicure chair, sat down at the chair, rolled up my pants, and dipped my feet into the tub, ready for the fun to begin.

I told her immediately that I wanted color. I showed her a picture of the OPI color I wanted called Girl Without Limits. They didn't carry it, but she brought me back four beautiful pink polishes. I chose Big Bow Energy, another gorgeous bright pink.

She trimmed my nails, filed them down, scrubbed my feet, massaged my legs, and painted my toes with multiple coats of base, that beautiful pink, and a hard topcoat. After about fifteen minutes, she came around and sprayed my toes to freeze the polish in place, helped me put on my flip flops, and I was out the door. I drove back to work but before I got back, I pulled over at a gas station to put my socks and shoes back on to hide my beautiful toes from the world . . . well, until the next day.

Atlanta

Friday, I got up before the crack of dawn . . . 4:00 a.m.! I got ready in guy mode, and covered my beautiful toes in socks and shoes, and went out the door. I made it through check-in and TSA checks without any hiccups. My plane took off about 7:00 a.m., and I arrived in Atlanta a couple hours later. I met up with Sami, one of the people I would be staying in a house with, at the airport and we got to know each other in guy mode. About thirty minutes later, our host, Meghan, picked us up from the airport, and we arrived at our Airbnb about an hour after that.

The house was so beautiful and located in a very LGBTQIA+ friendly area. Shortly after the tour of the house, we selected rooms, and I started unpacking all of my things for the weekend.

Next, I did something I had been dying to do for years—shave my legs!

Shaving my legs was amazing, but what I did not expect was how long it would take. First, it took about thirty minutes with my beard trimmer, then I got in the shower, lathered up my legs, and proceeded to shave each leg. I never expected this part of the process would take me an hour. After my legs were all smooth, I put a ton of lotion on them. They felt fantastic! Another hour later, I had on my daytime makeup, wig, and was doing what I loved to do—trying on my new dresses and taking pictures.

In the next couple hours, Aria, Olivia, and Olive and her wife started arriving. Then, it was time to add a little more makeup for my evening look and my new black summer jumper. After some group photos and a shot of coffee-flavored rum, we all piled into the minivan, and we were off. For dinner, we went to a unique horror-themed bar and grill called The Vortex. On the way in, people looked but did not stare, except when they were checking us out and giving us compliments. I chose a burger on the menu called Zombie Apocalypse. It had pulled pork and a sunny side egg on top. After eating that, along with tots and fried pickle sticks, I was stuffed.

After we let dinner settle for a moment, we piled back into the minivan. A few minutes later, we arrived at X Midtown, a drag bar. This was my first gay bar since college. We sat around and had a few drinks, and some nice chats, until the music started and the show began. It was so fun, and just about the perfect balance of raunchy, sexy, and funny. The show lasted a long time; when it ended, it was late. We ended up doing the smart thing, since it was Night One, and went back to the house to have a nightcap and chat.

When it was time for bed, I removed all my makeup and wig. I had planned to wear one of my wigs at night, but the top of my head hurt so much I could not even think about that. I put on my nightgown, slunk into the sheets with my freshly shaven legs, and curled up for a good night's sleep.

When I woke up Saturday morning, I walked downstairs in my nightgown and no wig and hung out with everyone. We watched College Game Day as we talked about football and other sports. After some breakfast sandwiches and tots, I got ready for the day.

The first event of the day was shopping. I put on some light makeup, a wig, jewelry, and my classic sundress, white with yellow and blue stripes. I had thought a lot about shopping in this dress, so after I put on my white satin corset, I zipped it up the back. I put on my new wedges, and I was ready to go.

We started at a thrift store called Out of the Closet, the perfect name for a LGBTQIA+ thrift store. It was a fun little thrift store, but even though I was the thrift-store queen, I came out empty-handed.

Next, we went to Little Five Points, a unique, eclectic area of town with tons of fun little shops. We went through a lot of shops! Most of it was not quite my style, but I had a great time. I did find one gorgeous long pink lace dress with a v-neck. I carried it around the store, but ended up putting it down instead of trying it on, because

I was worried it was too small, and that I might get stuck trying to pull it back over my wig.

The most memorable part of the shopping experience happened at the first store in Little Five Points. A beautiful cis woman came up to me and said, "I just have to tell you, I love your dress and it looks great on you!" It was *so* validating! After we had walked through every shop that looked interesting to us, we hopped back in the car to head back to the house.

When we arrived back at the house, most of the girls either took a nap or just relaxed. Not this girl! I was having too much fun, and wanted to bring out Jenn more. I had learned that modeling for the camera brings out Jenn better than just about anything, so I took a ton of pictures and videos.

When everyone started getting ready for the evening, I added my magnetic lashes and a little more makeup. Before the trip, I knew exactly the dress I wanted to wear out: my new bright pink, knee-length one. I also put on some nude pantyhose so my feet would slip a little easier into my shoes, and so I could experience them over my freshly shaven legs. One of the ladies had a friend join us for the evening. Her name was Aaron (Yes, she spells it *Aaron* and not *Erin*, because that is how she prefers it), and she was the only person who identified as transgender, fully presenting as female all of the time, but she fit right into our little group. After some group photos, it was time to pile into the minivan for a night of fun.

We started at the coolest lesbian night club called My Sister's Room. It was the perfect place to spend our last night. Upstairs held a dance club, and the first floor was a totally different dance club that—as the evening progressed—turned into a drag show. Outside, there was a large space with tables, chairs, etc., which was the perfect place to chill.

That is where we began our night. We all ate too many fried foods. This was one of my favorite parts of the weekend, because we had the most amazing conversations. With a little encouragement, I even brought out my Jenn voice because I am not fully her without it. It made the night a lot better.

Before I went on the trip, I had been inspired by Aaron, the trans woman who joined us. It just happened that we were sitting directly across from each other. I told Aaron about how inspiring her Instagram posts were, and that I was excited to meet her in person.

There was something so welcoming about Aaron that brought out my vulnerable side and I asked her all kinds of questions and told her all about me and my journey. During our conversations, I realized how incredibly similar our stories were, which was scary and comforting at the same time.

We had the best, but toughest, conversation I ever had talking about my gender journey. I shared that one of my counselors asked me, "If tomorrow you were single without kids, what would you do?" I told her I would dabble in hormone-replacement therapy (HRT) immediately.

She said she felt the exact same way for a long time. As she told me about her journey, tears started running down my face. Our stories were incredibly similar.

"I think I am transgender," I finally said aloud.

She replied gently, "From what you have told me, I think you are, too."

Next, we moved inside to the top bar for dancing. We danced and danced. During one of the songs, people started doing the electric slide. I knew the dance, so I joined in as I was here to take advantage of every opportunity this weekend. After some more dancing, we all started moving slower, and decided it was time to take this party back to the house.

The journey back to the minivan was a challenging one. I remember stumbling back and forth, not because I had too much to drink, but because my feet hurt so bad, and my legs were in so much pain.

After we got back to the house, someone said, "Let's all do karaoke!" We did two rounds each. The rule was if you skipped, you had to take a shot.

My first round was embarrassing. Somehow, I thought it was a good idea to try to do both voices of "Barbie Girl" by Aqua. Let's just say, it is a good thing we agreed on no video. (LOL!) For my second song, I chose "I Want It That Way" by Backstreet Boys. It was a much better choice as it was manageable, and everyone joined in. After everyone had done their two rounds, we finished the night in the perfect way . . . Olive introduced us to country singer Orville Peck's version of the song "Born This Way." As we sang along, I literally felt in every ounce of my being that I was *born this way*.

The next morning, after about four hours of sleep, I woke up and proceeded to pack up to head home. After I was all packed, I headed downstairs where we chatted a bit and said our goodbyes. Sami and I put our bags in Olivia's car and we left for the airport. Once through security, we said our goodbyes and I proceeded to my gate where I sat down, reflected, messaged my new sisters, and wrote all about the trip.

https://www.jennspire.com/15-atlanta

Accepting Myself

After I returned home from Atlanta, I had a counseling session that week. I told Counselor #4 all about the trip, but most of what we focused on was my conversation with Aaron, and how it rocked me so much I had tears streaming down my face. I told her I was questioning whether I was transgender harder than ever. She told me, "When you have time this week, I want you to do an exercise called fear-setting."

In fear-setting, you identify your fear, name the worst things that could happen, and identify the best steps to fix each of them. Then you lay out all the positives if you were to conquer your fear.

I completed the exercise, and I only could think of four potential negatives for transitioning, but when it came to creating a list of positives, I came up with *eight*. I had double the positives compared to the potential negatives. I was filled with joy!

Aaron and I continued to talk after I left Atlanta. One night she and I were talking, and she told me I needed to read a book called *Untamed* by Glennon Doyle. She said if you do not have time to read the book, you need to at least read the prologue. The next day I found the audio book and listened in my car. I was so glad I was in a private, safe place when I listened.

The prologue is about a cheetah named Tabitha that was born in captivity. The cheetah was taught by Minnie, a dog that was her best friend. After the dog would do a trick, the cheetah would do the same trick and then receive her prize of a juicy steak. When Glennon saw this happen, she didn't clap . . . it was all too *familiar*. . . this taming. One of the kids asked, "Isn't Tabitha sad? Doesn't she miss the wild?" To which they received the response, "No. Tabitha was born here. She doesn't know any different. She's never even seen the wild. This is a good life for Tabitha. She's much safer here than she would be out in the wild."

Tears began to form in my eyes.

A little bit later, Glennon's daughter got her attention as she could see the cheetah as it was away from everyone.

> There, in that field, away from Minnie and the zookeepers, Tabitha's posture had changed. Her head was high, and

she was stalking the periphery, tracing the boundaries the fence created. Back and forth, back and forth, stopping only to stare somewhere beyond the fence. It was like she was remembering something. She looked regal, and a little scary."

Tish (Glennon's daughter) whispered to me, "Mommy, she turned wild again."

Hearing those words, I burst into hard sobbing tears for several minutes. Like Glennon, this was all too familiar, I just never realized it until that moment. I had led a sheltered life, and raised as a boy I never seriously considered anything differently, even though the signs were there all along.

That day I surrendered and accepted myself completely as a proud transgender woman and knew I had to make some changes in my life!

Coming Out Online

I have always loved watching children's animated movies, especially Disney and Pixar films, even before I had kids. I always enjoyed them, but as I was discovering myself, I found that some of their newer films meant a lot more to me. Many times, I found myself tearing up at the story, or the songs, because of how they related to my life.

I began an Instagram series where one-by-one, I shared each of those movies that had an impact on me. One of them was "Turning

Red," the story of a girl that learns that she is also a red panda, but it can be controlled. She can hide it from the world forever, but in the end she realizes that doing so she would be giving up a huge piece of herself, and decides to keep her panda.

Every time I watched this movie with my kids, I had tears in my eyes. I know I could have lived a life where I just hid my identity away, but like the main character in the movie, I did not want to lose a huge piece of myself, so I did not get rid of my "panda" either.

The final post of the series was my anthem that my inner girl was screaming out at me for so long: Frozen's "Let it Go." It was time to let it *all* go and I shared with my 20,000 followers, "I'm transgender and proud of it!"

Meeting My Sister

Now that I had decided to slowly begin to transition, I wanted my sister to meet the real me. She liked the idea, so we planned out a fun night of drag and drinking.

On that special night, I met up with my friend Josie and her wife and got ready with them in their hotel room. I put on a black top and some jeans, along with my wig, makeup, accessories, and a new purse that I bought for the occasion. I wanted to wear a dress and never felt complete in pants, but I did not want to overwhelm my sister, so I wore pants.

When we arrived at the venue, we proceeded to the table where my sister and her boyfriend were waiting for us. Neither of them flinched, and she gave me a big hug. She referred to me as Jenn all night without hesitation and her boyfriend and I just chatted, just like we had done in the past. It was just so perfectly normal. After the drag show was over, we proceeded to another bar where Josie had friends waiting for her to stop by.

As we walked in Josie and I were waved over to join them at their table. They were both incredibly beautiful! Sitting down and talking with them, it immediately felt like home. They immediately felt like family. My sister could see it too, so we hugged and said our goodbyes, as she knew I was in good hands.

I was with my people, so I immediately started telling them everything about my journey. They were both so supportive! Our conversations continued to confirm I was on the right path, and I added three sisters that night to my amazing family!

https://www.jennspire.com/16-meeting-my-sister

Chapter Seven

Jenn Ascending

As the conversations with my wife continued, I had hoped and prayed that progress would be made. I kept hearing on repeat how it was a sin, a form of sexual addiction, and so on. I needed my wife to show some sign that she was trying to understand me, and that there was something to work toward.

A few months before, I told her, "I need you to show me you are trying, even with something small, to be able to get to a point where if you bought yourself a lip gloss that you could buy me one." She informed me this was offensive, and couldn't believe I would say that to her.

One night, after the kids were in bed, I said, "A few months ago, I told you I need you to show me you are trying, even with something small, to be able to get to a point where if you bought yourself a lip gloss that you could buy me one. That day you told me it was offensive that I would say that. Do you still feel this way?"

Her response was exactly the same. I even remember her elaborating and reminding me that she doesn't change her mind on anything.

Unfortunately, I knew this to be true. It was done. We were over. I knew what I had to say, though I had hoped and prayed I would never have to say it. Drawing a deep breath, I looked at her intently.

"Then we don't work," I said calmly. "You hate at least half of who I am."

Within the coming weeks, we had mostly cordial conversations about separation, and what we both would like to see in a divorce. Talking about not being with the woman that I loved—and the woman who had been my best friend for many years—was extremely difficult.

Most of our conversations revolved around the kids. We both were on the same page with most things. We both wanted to co-parent well for the kids, so we planned to live in the same area, send the kids to the same school, and we both wanted her to keep the house. We also wanted as much cohesiveness and little change for the kids as possible.

Then, we started talking about the stuff we both had been avoiding. We both knew each of us had called attorneys to represent us in a divorce, because I called one that she had met with. She knew I put down a five-thousand dollar deposit with my attorney, because she had seen our checking account statement. She was upset because she thought I was just going to serve her without any warning.

She asked if I was going to tell my parents. She insisted that they needed to know that our marriage ending was not her fault.

I just nodded and agreed. It was so hard *not* to come out and tell her that I already had told them, but by now things had changed between us. This was the person I shared every single innermost thought with . . . and now she was no longer my person. Heading into divorce, I did not feel safe to share anything with her anymore.

She asked if I was going to tell my new employer. I kind of skirted the question, and said I am currently trying to find a more accepting employer, so if it comes out, they will be more likely to accept me.

Then, she mentioned she was going to start laser-hair removal on her upper lip. I told her in the spirit of our renewed open communication, "I started laser hair removal on my face." I told her about my experience, and welcomed her to go to my place. It made her sad to lose that part of me. She expressed that she was worried that one day she would look at me and not see me anymore. *I expect one day that will be true,* and while that made me happy for myself, I was also saddened that it upset her.

As we finished the conversation, she said she wanted to continue to talk about things, but not make any agreements without attorneys, as it will save money for both of us. I agreed that it would be a great idea, so long as we could continue our communication in the manner that we were experiencing currently.

Unfortunately, this rarely works, and we were no different . . .

The Wedding Dress

As I hinted at earlier when I talked about my wedding, a beautiful wedding dress was something I always dreamed of wearing. Like a lot of little girls, they daydream of wearing one and looking forward to that day; I was no different.

When I was planning on staying with my wife, my fantasy was to get remarried as two brides. I knew it was a fantasy, as I felt she would be disgusted at the thought, so I decided I was going to make my fantasy come true, at least to some extent.

I had spent countless hours admiring wedding dresses online and imagining myself wearing them. One day in April 2022, I found a beautiful, never worn Maggie Sottero wedding dress on Poshmark that I realized—after taking some measurements—was perfect! It was calling out to me, as it was only $120. . . so I bought it!

A couple of weeks later, I picked it up at the post office. It was all boxed up and I knew there was not going to be an opportunity to wear it, or even get it out to look at, so I put it away in my safe. It killed me to not be able to wear it yet. I thought about it every day until I tried it months later, while everyone was out of the house. Since I did not have time to get all dolled up, I put it on in guy mode and used Faceapp to feminize my face with filters so that I could stand to look at the pictures.

As I waited in anticipation for the day that I could wear it all dolled up, I started planning. I was going to create a faux wedding, and invite some of my friends from Instagram to come be bridesmaids.

I even thought about finding a guy to stand in as my groom. I had a lot of fun planning this. I talked to a couple of friends about it who were excited about the idea and opportunity to be a bridesmaid. The day I stopped planning was the day I decided I was going to transition. I knew transitioning meant starting a new life after divorce; I had high hopes that one day I would get remarried as the woman I am, and then I would finally get to be the bride!

Deciding to transition did not stop my desire to wear the dress, however. One weekend in November, I had the house to myself, so I got all dolled up and took pictures. It was mostly a happy feeling. Wearing the dress with full makeup, along with the wedding jewelry, veil, and ivory peep-toe kitten heels (that were too tight) I had purchased felt great. There were three things bothering me, though.

One, I was still struggling with hiding my five o'clock shadow. Two, I was tired of hiding. Dressing in private started feeling fake. I wanted to be in public. Three, I wanted to be wearing this wedding dress for real. That is why I canceled my plans. I did not want a faux wedding. I want it to be real . . . *all of it!*

https://www.jennspire.com/17-the-wedding-dress

Meeting My Friends

As I previously mentioned, one of the first people I came out to was Sam, one of my friends from high school. He was supportive from day one, and we continued to talk. One day, Sam mentioned he would be coming back home to celebrate the holidays with his mother. I told him I would love to find time for him to meet the real me. He was excited, so we planned it.

I bought a new dress for the occasion, not just because I wanted to, but I needed a long-sleeved dress because I did not have one. I also bought a long women's dress coat and fleece-lined tights. Why? The temperature here was below zero! It was the coldest day of the year, but nothing was going to stop this night from happening.

I met up at my friend Jess T's place to get ready, as I could not get ready at home. My amazing friend Ash braved the cold to come along as my support. I was so excited for this night that I had been thinking about it for months. I had used the word "giddy" earlier in the day texting Sam. I was especially giddy, because Sam's partner was joining us, along with Andrew, one of my friends from high school who did not know I was trans. I was going to surprise him. He had no idea who they were meeting. This was going to be fun!

After a couple hours, Ash and I were ready to go. We drove to the restaurant and as we parked in front my friends came walking up the sidewalk. They almost walked past me until I said, "Hi guys."

Andrew was shocked . . . yet not shocked, knowing me and how much I dressed.

The night was amazing! I shared my entire story and they all asked great questions. I have always loved answering any question from people who want to learn more about me, or trans issues in general. The thing I was not prepared for was the amount of love and support they showered me with! I was even more unprepared for how they treated me, because of my social media following. They made me feel kind of like a celebrity and it made me feel really special. To go from being bullied and feeling like nothing to the pretty girl everyone wanted to talk to was just the best feeling. It was a magical night, and one I will never forget!

https://www.jennspire.com/18-meeting-my-friends

A New Way to Coexist

As I was preparing for divorce, I had some big thoughts and ideas. I wrote another letter to my wife:

I know you can tell I'm changing a lot. The truth is I recently realized I am a woman and need to live as one. I do still love you and would love to be with you, but I understand if this is a deal breaker for you.

I was thinking about divorce, and I got to thinking . . . that's not at all what I want. I know it sounds crazy, but hear me out and think about it.

What if we did this? We get separated, but live in this house as two great co-parents? I can make the playroom into my bedroom. We will still share the same bathroom and closet, but my other stuff lives in my new closet. I will continue supporting us and we will share assets for at least until the kids' next school year. Before next school year, we decide whether we want a divorce, whether this setup works, whether you get a full-time job, etc.

We both love our kids, and don't want to give up any time with them, and we both love this house. I believe this is a way we could have both. It's not perfect, but I'm willing to work on it with you if you are willing to.

I have an appointment at the end of November to start on hormones. I tell you this because I want to be as honest and forward as I have been. When I know something, as difficult as it is for both of us, I share it with you.

I know all of this is a lot. I encourage you to go pamper yourself for a day. Just let me know when and I'll watch the kids.

You were my best friend and I need you back, even if you can't be my partner. The truth is I am nervous, even though I know I'm doing what I have to.

I never gave her that letter. I wanted to so badly, but I felt like she would never agree and even more I could not take the chance she would use any of it against me in divorce.

Big Local Weekend

As we were headed into divorce, I felt the need to be more and more myself. I became more honest about when I needed girl time, something I had rarely done. I told my wife I was leaving for the

124

weekend, but the truth is I just stayed in town. I knew it would save money and I had a lot of friends I wanted to meet up with, so I just rented a room downtown.

Friday, I slept in and did some shopping, mostly for a skirt and tights. I never imagined how difficult it would be to find skirts in person that are not juniors, but I found a cute one at Kohls and bought it.

After I checked into my hotel and got situated, after taking three trips from the car to get all my stuff to the room, I tried on a ton of clothes I had bought recently. After I made my selections, it was time to get ready for the evening. I chose my new skirt with a black bodysuit, black tights, and black stilettos, along with my new necklace and some clip-on earrings.

Everything was close by, but not close enough to walk so I Ubered. I met up with Ash and Jess T for sushi and sake. After our delicious meal, it was time for dancing.

We hopped in the car and headed to a gay club. The only thing that surprised me was how many straight people were there, but everyone was so nice! We danced until our stilettos hurt, took a break, and repeated. We had a great time! Toward the end of the night, I got hit on in the cutest way by a girl at the club.

"I just want to say I have been loving your look all night and if I wasn't here with my serious girlfriend, I would be all over you," she said. "I know it probably sounds kind of weird, but it's a compliment." I told her I loved it! She was sweet!

After our feet were shot, my friends dropped me off at my place and we chatted for a long time before I got out of the car. It was late, but I did not want to leave them, as they are amazing. There was nothing better than connecting with other girls like me. I removed all my clothes and makeup and could not stop smiling. What a great night! I put on my cute pjs and curled up in my bed.

I woke up Saturday well rested and happy. I just had a great night and was ready for an exciting day of firsts! After getting ready in my skinny jeans, sweater, and tall black boots, I was off to meet my sister for a wig fitting.

I walked into the shop and was immediately greeted with a warm welcome. The staff was so nice and respectful! We even used a privacy curtain, which made me more comfortable. It was so great having my sister there for support and she had some great input as well. After talking about styles I might be interested in, the wig specialist took me to the wall, and I picked out several I wanted to try. I ended up selecting one of the first ones I tried on. When she found it in a lighter shade, I knew this was it!

As I was checking out, the stylist told me to come back soon, and she would teach me how to take great care of my wig, along with all kinds of great styling tips. My sister had to leave, but that was alright, as it meant a new first for me was coming . . . eating out by myself.

After I wore my new wig out of the store, giving me so much confidence, my stomach was talking to me, so I found a place nearby for brunch. I walked in and everyone was so nice! I got a few looks, but I am a tall girl, and I was owning it!

After a bacon avocado omelet, toast, some little potatoes, and an iced coffee, I realized my feet were killing me. My boots were rubbing the back of my foot, so I hopped in the car and found a Target nearby. I had never been in a store as Jenn, so I told myself with my new confidence *I do not care what store this is or how many people are here . . . I can do this!*

I walked in and received some looks, probably mostly because I was hobbling as my foot was in extreme pain. As I was walking in, I had to use the restroom, so I figured time for another first. I only saw a couple women inside the restroom, but neither one looked at me. I got back to the car and took my boots off. Sure enough, I had worn through several layers of skin. I applied some medicine and bandages on my foot. I was in so much pain, I decided to skip shopping and head back to the room to rest.

After a long nap, it was time to get ready for the night. I tried on several dresses and settled on the one I thought about not even bringing, but I loved it on me. It was a tight black dress with a design on the front. It was hugging me in all the right places.

The Italian restaurant I was meeting my friend at was only a few blocks away, but I figured it was best to Uber, as it is probably not the safest for me to walk five blocks in stilettos. As I walked in, everyone turned and looked at me, but I looked hot and owned it!

The food was amazing, and I loved the company I was with. We had risotto balls, lasagna, and focaccia bread, and I had a glass of chardonnay. (Yes, wine lover reading this, I should have paired it with a red, but it was a special night and I wanted my favorite wine.) After some great food and conversation, my friend dropped me back at my hotel. I curled up and relished the amazing day I just had.

I woke up smiling on Sunday with breasts, as this was the first time I slept with my bra and chicken cutlet breast forms on. I packed up my things and went back to boy mode, which was continuing to get more difficult each time. I decided I was going to focus on the amazing weekend I had, which put a smile on my face as I walked out the door carrying my new wig.

https://www.jennspire.com/19-big-local-weekend

Last Father-Son Moment

Earlier in the week, my father invited me to a football game. It was special, as I knew it would be the last father and son time together before I started my medical transition three days later.

It was typical of our times going together, except I was thinking about being a woman the entire time. I was focusing more on what girls were wearing, how they cheered or clapped, etc. I began to imitate them, secretly.

We tailgated with some of his church friends. I loved that one of the girls at the tailgate was almost as tall as me, which made me feel even better about transitioning at my height. After some great drinks and food, we walked to the stadium for the game. It was an entertaining game and just like old times, we were high fiving after touchdowns and talking about the game.

On the way home, I thanked him for bringing me. "I'm really glad we were able to do this today," I explained. "Because things are going to start changing with me . . . and I know it will take some time, but I hope one day we can do stuff like this again."

"It is hard, because I don't understand it," he replied gently. "I think you are giving up a lot."

And we left it at that. It was a great day, so I chalked it up as a win.

HRT

As I had planned since I stopped denying I was transgender, I was starting gender-affirming hormone replacement therapy (most of us call it HRT for short.) Within a day of making that life-changing decision to transition, I called and made an appointment with a local gender clinic so I could start HRT.

I had my current counselor write a letter in case I needed it. The process was relatively easy after they diagnosed me with gender dysphoria.

"We'll start you on six milligrams of estradiol to increase your estrogen levels," the doctor explained.

"I'm still living with my wife who cannot know about any of this yet," I replied. "I don't want physical results right now. I want the internal results. I want to feel right within my body. I am interested in a low dose. I was thinking two milligrams per day."

"You can do that, but that dosage is usually reserved for non-binary," she explained. "For your diagnosis, four milligrams is considered a low dose."

I agreed to start there, taking four milligrams of estradiol in tablet form daily, in addition to the two hundred milligrams of Spironolactone to suppress my testosterone levels. I was excited, and went straight to the pharmacy. Once I picked up my prescriptions, I took both medications immediately.

At this time, I was still living with my wife. Before I moved out and called it quits, I wanted to know if I felt right within my body. If not, I was ready to regroup, and not give up on us.

It took me less than two weeks to feel right within my body for the first time in my life. I felt happier, calmer, and more settled than I had ever felt.

But it was also bittersweet, because I knew I had to move out.

Preparing for Divorce

We lived in a conservative state, and I had read horror stories of transgender parents losing custody in their divorce over their choice to live as their true selves. I could not let that happen to me.

In case it was to get ugly in my divorce where my identity was brought up, I knew I needed an attorney who had represented a transgender person in a divorce before. I used my large supportive network, especially those who were attorneys, and followed up on every referral. Many of them were not taking on new cases, and some became unavailable after I told them I was trans. At first that was frustrating, but I quickly realized if they did not want to represent me because I was trans, then they were not the right person.

After many calls, I found *him*. He was an attorney who was highly recommended by a friend who got a referral from a Democratic politician. He had been involved in transgender divorce cases before, he was confident and friendly, and he was gay, which I also loved. During our first call he told me I needed to delete or make all my traces of Jenn online private, so I reluctantly did.

I made my Instagram and Facebook private, not letting anyone in unless I knew them well. Then, I removed my profile pic and put up an avatar of myself, removed my content from my blog, etc. It was really difficult because I was living online, and Jenn was being trapped in this little box. I stopped posting personal things. I mostly posted pretty pictures and videos for the next year, just in case my wife or someone she knew was already following me.

Next, something much more difficult happened. I received an email from the law office that said my attorney was leaving the practice, and due to his non-compete, he would no longer be able to represent me. I remember breaking down and crying. I had searched so hard to find him and just like happened at my first counselor, I was going to have to start the process all over again.

When I spoke with my attorney on the phone, he told me they had other attorneys in the practice who could represent me. I told him I wanted the best attorney that would be able to represent me in my special situation.

He thought about it for a second, and suggested a straight cis local attorney with her own small law firm. "She is the best at mediating a difficult situation," he assured me.

She had never represented a trans person before, but she was very accepting. When I met with her, I really liked her but her never having represented a person like me, made me nervous. I did not have another option, so she represented me throughout the divorce process.

Anger and Hate

"What are we doing for Christmas?" I began. "Like, are we each giving separate presents to the kids, or are we giving them together?"

She asked what I wanted to do about it, or whether I had any thoughts on it.

Since I still considered it 'our' money, giving presents together made the most sense. This was met with almost a guarded resignation, it seemed; we both knew this year was somewhat different, but I still wanted to celebrate as a family . . . even though I had to hear once again about how I broke up our family because I continued to search out and explore who I was.

Arguments with my wife were typically rooted in love, but this one was different. It was rooted in anger.

"I have been searching for answers my entire life," I replied, trying to remain calm. "I should have figured it out before I started dating you and for that, I am sorry. I had no idea I was going to end up here. Shame is a powerful thing."

She snapped and indicated we would never be friends again because she can't trust me.

Next, she asked about my plans for the future: where I would be 'her,' how far I was going to take this, what I was going to tell my parents, etc.

"I haven't figured it all out yet," I retorted, starting to feel a lump in my throat with my blood pressure rising at the same time. "But you don't want anything to do with that side of me, so it doesn't concern you."

I could feel the anger in her response. She insisted that it does concern her because of our children, that she needs to be prepared, and prepare the children for what is going to happen.

I just shrugged my shoulders. While I wanted to tell her more, it didn't feel safe to do so.

The conversation wasn't over yet. She wasn't done.

She continued next saying in what felt like a combative tone that lasering my face was an insult to her because little by little

I was taking away the things that make me different from her permanently. She explained that because those things are different, they are the things that she loves.

"It has nothing to do with you," I shot back, exhausted from the multitude of times I'd said that line. "Making these changes is not fun for me—it's not just something I *like* to do, or am doing to spite you. I'm doing the laser-hair removal because I hate seeing hair on my face. I can't be her because the stubble drives me crazy."

The discussion about Christmas continued. We couldn't play pretend anymore—that was the takeaway I received from my wife.

"I'm not pretending. I said I don't hate you," I replied calmly.

With hostility in her tone, she wanted to know why I would hate her, because *she* hadn't done anything to *me*.

"You want to blame me for everything, but I have evolved and found who I am, and you want nothing to do with the other side of me."

She asked what I expected.

"As I have explained in previous conversations, I want you to be friends with her (my other side)," I said calmly.

She informed me that she didn't want a girlfriend and that she wanted a husband!

"I want both."

She yelled that I couldn't have both.

"Not in this marriage," I replied, and walked away.

Getting Along

Shortly after that last hateful conversation, I wrote this in my journal:

Last two days have been good at home with my wife. It's great to get along, but it makes it that much more difficult because of what I have to do. I'm so emotional right now because I know that I need to file for divorce in a few days. I so badly want to tell her I'm trans and transitioning and I am still crazy about her and want to make this work, but I can't. I can't for three reasons:

1. *Custody battle would be much harder. I want equal time with my kids.*
2. *She doesn't want anything to do with Jenn. Can't even learn her name nor want to be part of her life.*
3. *Three little letters . . . HRT. I can't go back to being him now, and I don't want to. Estrogen courses through my veins, and I love it. While it makes me feel fatigued, I haven't been this alive in years and I haven't felt at peace within myself ever.*

I know who I am and there is no going back, but it doesn't make it any easier.

It Gets Really Ugly

I started getting results from the HRT much quicker than I ever anticipated, or even wanted. I was on a low dose and my body was so ready for it, it started changing. Here is a summary of the first month.

Week One

Within the first day, I started experiencing tiny piercing pains in my back. The pains continued for most of the rest of the week, and then the fatigue started to set in. I was so much more tired than I had ever been. I slept for a full eight hours consistently and still woke up tired. My taste in food even started to change a little bit.

Week Two

As the second week began, I felt like I could eat a *cow*. I was so hungry and had to make myself stop eating. This continued for months. Also, in the second week, my friend who I talked to every day, noticed that I was becoming a little more girly each time we talked. She could tell it just by talking to me on the phone.

Week Three

As the third week began, my nipples started itching. I also noticed myself moving more femininely. For the last few months, when no one was looking, I had been trying to force my feminine posture and mannerisms to feel more like Jenn, but now those things were coming naturally. I was sitting in a chair and my legs naturally tucked underneath me and my arms crossed in a feminine way. I was loving every part of it, but I had to start being aware not to draw attention to myself.

Week Four

As the fourth week began, I noticed my nipples were not itching anymore, but were getting more sensitive—and my breasts started to ache. In addition to aching, my nipples were budding (getting little dots all over them), and they started protruding. This is when I started wearing a bralette under my shirt every day to hide my pointy enlarged nipples.

It was around that fourth week that I became self-conscious and was really nervous my ex was going to figure it out. She would walk by me while I was showering. Then I noticed she was getting ready at a much slower pace than usual at the vanity outside the shower. One day, as I was getting out of the shower, she came running into the bathroom. I quickly grabbed my towel and wrapped it around my upper body. I then proceeded to the master closet to get some clothes.

She followed me there, moving closer and closer and was staring at me, just standing there. Nervously, but as calmly as I could say it, I said "Excuse me, but could I please get some privacy?"

In colorful terms, I was advised that I do not get any privacy in my own home.

"Fine, then I'll go somewhere where I do," I said dismissively. Grabbing my clothes, I walked into the toilet room and locked the door. My heart pounded, but I got dressed in peace.

That day I decided that would never happen again, so I joined a local gym mostly to have a place to shower in peace. After a couple days of this, she informed me I could shower in the guest bathroom.

The next day I started locking the door and showering in the guest bathroom.

After that, I started to become paranoid. I felt like I was being followed. Before things started getting too crazy at home, I moved my HRT medications from my car to my storage unit, where I had moved all my clothing, shoes, accessories, makeup, etc., months prior. I moved it just in time before I noticed things were out of place in my car. Next, I felt like someone was following me. I immediately stopped going to my storage unit and just did without my HRT pills. As all this drama was unfolding, I realized I needed to get out of that house ASAP!

https://www.jennspire.com/20-it-gets-really-ugly

Moving Out

Moving out was very emotional for me. Not only had I put my blood, sweat, and tears into renovating our dream home, I was essentially saying goodbye to the life I had with my wife of twelve years.

I wrote the following on Instagram:

Today marks the last week. The last week of what? The last week of living at home with my wife. I appreciate everyone's support and cheering us on. And while I am excited to be able to be the person I was born to be, it's also really sad that I can't do it with my partner by my side. It's going to be a really hard week for both of us, so as I've asked before, please send prayers and positive thoughts our way this week. It's going to be a very difficult, but necessary week for all of us.

That Friday night, I told the kids I was moving out and not coming back; I made it clear, however, they will have a home with me and have everything they need.

Their reaction was amazing! The kids focused on two things: one, they couldn't wait to come see my house, and two, will I have good toys for them to play with?

The next day was the move. Everything went well, and while exhausting, I was out. I surprisingly didn't get too emotional as I said goodbye. It helped that my wife and kids were not there. I teared up as I said goodbye to our dog, and walked out the door for the last time. The next feeling I had was excitement. I was excited to start living my life and not have to ask permission to be myself. I was free!

Chapter Eight

Early Transition

I want to share something with you, so you can understand how different of a place I was in after I moved out. Here's an entry I wrote in my journal about a week and a half after I moved out:

I moved out of the home my wife and I built together for about twelve years, which in a lot of ways was one of the hardest things I have ever done, and while I cherish most of those memories, I do not regret leaving for one second. I have never been happier or taken better care of myself.

When I was married, I put her needs before my own, including my identity. I never did a deep dive into why I continually have this desire to present as a woman, even though that desire, and honestly need, has been there my entire life. Looking back at it, I think I was just scared, scared of losing what I had but, in the end, the scariest part was I was beginning to lose myself.

So, I took action. I wrote out my story, I reached out to people like me, and I have never looked back, because I realized it's time to take care of me.

I started seeing therapists who understood me, pushed me, and allowed me to find the better version of myself. I found people in my life that pushed me, too. Towards the end of 2022, I found someone online that essentially is me, but twenty years older, and regrets all the years that she missed out on being her true self. I do not regret any part of my life, but I am so freaking excited for my next twenty years.

Like I said, I am taking better care of myself, and I owe a huge part of that to my new friend that is an almost identical version of me. She is amazing! She pushes me every day to be a better version of myself, because she knows who I am, what I want and how to get there. She played a huge part in helping me find a place, so I could get out of that house, and convinced me that even though I thought I wanted a house to rent, Jenn would never want to be working in the yard. She's right. That's not me. Not anymore. She pushed me to eat healthier. I stopped buying frozen meals and more than ever I am trying to eat a balanced diet. One, so I look good, but mostly, it's for my health. She pushed me to start exercising. She bought me a yoga mat and encouraged me to try a Barre workout she likes on YouTube. I did and it rocks my body every time I do it, but I feel better. I feel better because I am taking care of my body, which is giving me energy and a drive I haven't had in a long time. I am currently working with some key people to find a job with an employer that will embrace the true me.

I have lived on my own for eleven days already and being back on HRT, eating right, dressing how I want to frequently, working out, and preparing for my future, I have hardly ever been happier. That's just eleven days . . . I can't wait to see where I end up!

Saturday As Me

The next Saturday was an amazing, affirming day. I put on panties and a bra under my male clothes, as I had done most days since

I started HRT, and moved to my own house. Saturday morning was the court-required, one-time co-parenting class that I had to attend. I was counting down the time for the session to end—not because I hated the class, but because of what I had planned for that afternoon.

When the clock struck noon, I hurried home and started getting ready. I took a quick shower, dried off, and started preparing my entire body to present as my true self for the afternoon.

About 2:30 p.m., I arrived at the wig shop, where I had purchased my nice wig on that euphoric day a few months back. As you may recall, when I purchased my wig, she said she could teach me how to take care of it and all kinds of tips and tricks. I remember telling her I would come back when my wig could have a home on a wig stand in my closet. This was the first Saturday since I moved, so I took advantage of the opportunity.

From washing to styling, she taught me everything. I learned so much! I had no idea that a quality synthetic wig could be styled with hot tools, such as a curling iron. After she taught me all she could, and I asked every question I could think of, I bought a mannequin head, stand, shampoo and conditioner, so I could take care of my wig at home. As I was leaving, I noticed my sister had texted me.

She asked me if I wanted to meet up with her and her boyfriend for drinks. I was thrilled! They both were super nice to me as they always were, no matter how I was presenting. We had good drinks, great conversation, and then it was time for us to go our separate ways. I was not ready for my special day to end, so I decided to do a little shopping.

I had recently purchased a coffee maker that also had an espresso maker attached. What better time than now to stop by a specialty store I loved and pick up a couple espresso cups? I walked in and everyone looked at me, and then they went about their business, as usual. I made my purchase and then decided I would much rather take home dinner than make dinner that night, so I picked up a salad.

Everything in the restaurant went so smoothly. No one stared, and I was even called "ma'am" by the lady who handed me my food. I loved every minute of it. I took my salad home with a smile on my face.

It was another affirming day in the books; one day, I knew such experiences would be common. I looked forward to that day.

https://www.jennspire.com/21-earlytransition-saturdayasme

Asheville

A few months after the trip to Atlanta, I was invited to go on another trip with the girls from Instagram. All of the girls from the previous trip would be there, and some new faces would be joining us as well. I could not pass up the opportunity, so I accepted.

I arrived in Asheville, North Carolina, and—after a little bit of playing phone tag to find our group—we finally met up and headed to the house. It was so good to see all of the girls from the Atlanta trip, and great meeting the three new ladies. The house was beautiful and spacious! With the exception of a couple girls sleeping in a bunk room of full-sized beds, we each got our own rooms. I selected one of the master suites away from everyone else, and felt like a princess in her own castle.

While some of the ladies hung out and talked, I hurried off to my bathroom to shave my entire body and transform. I put on my black Lululemon leggings and hot pink North Face hoodie. Complete with my wig and makeup, I felt cute.

After a little bit of hanging out with the girls, it was time to get ready for the night. I wore my sexy short little black dress and black pumps with black pantyhose, because it was cold. I also put on my black coat and joined the group. When I got outside, I was so glad I had my coat! It was about 20 degrees, and the wind was blowing so hard, it was howling. It was a rough walk to the club from the van in the cold wind. It was a very chilly club upstairs, but they had tacos. And I was hungry!

We chatted, danced a little bit, and called it a night. When we arrived back at the house, I removed my makeup, put on my silk light pink pjs, and was ready for a good night's sleep.

I woke up Saturday morning feeling refreshed. I walked over to the other side of the house to see what the girls were doing. A few of them were watching TV, a few were still sleeping, and a few had just finished their breakfast. A small group decided to play disc golf. I had never played disc golf, but my goal for the weekend was to get out publicly as much as possible, and it sounded fun. I ate a quick breakfast sandwich, changed back into my leggings and hoodie from the day before, and threw on a pair of white tennis shoes. A quick application of lip gloss and a new cute stocking cap were the final touches before I joined the rest of the group.

When we arrived at the course, I had no idea that I was not dressed appropriately. While everyone else wore more hiking-type shoes, I wore slip-on tennis shoes. I had expected the course to be in an open field, kind of like golf, but the course was in the woods. It was beautiful, but way more like hiking in the woods than golf. It took me several holes to figure it out, but I got the hang of it, and had a great time.

We grabbed lunch to-go and ate at the house. While we were eating, one of the girls mentioned she wanted to go shoe shopping. I told her if she wanted company, I'd love to go. I just needed a few minutes to apply some makeup, and then I'd be ready. I put on some light makeup and my wig, and in about twenty minutes, I was ready. She had decided to go get ready herself, so I hung out with some of the girls overlooking the lake.

When she was ready, a couple of us climbed in the car and we headed for the stores. We first hit Ross. She found three pairs of shoes she liked, and then we wandered back to the dresses. I found a cute light pink Calvin Klein dress that would be good for date night and work. I decided to try it on, and I proceeded to the women's fitting rooms for my first time, which felt right. I went into the stall and tried it on. It fit me like a glove, so I bought it.

Next, we went to Dillard's. I didn't find anything, but just enjoyed the experience. This was my first time as my true self at a mall and there were people everywhere but other than a quick glance they went about their business . . . just as it should be.

The entire weekend went so smoothly, I do not remember much else. I know we went to a club, but I do not remember anything about it, because that's not what that weekend was for me. That weekend gave me the opportunity to just exist and be in public as me in a safe space. It's why I tagged along to everything I could.

The trip was totally different from the Atlanta trip, but it was perfect. As I was sitting in the airport, I started getting emotional. I had such a great weekend with so many amazing girls from all over the country on different parts of the gender spectrum, but we all formed a bond that may last a lifetime. While a little scary, I was ready to come out and be my true self . . . the only thing holding me back was securing a new role with an accepting employer, *and* the blessing from my attorney.

https://www.jennspire.com/22-earlytransition-asheville

Battle to Find the Right Employer

Before I began the part of my journey where I really started diving into the why and figuring myself out, I was with the same employer. Jokes and comments about transgender and non-binary people ran rampant in my office. As I realized who I was, I began to take those comments more personally than ever, but I could not let anyone know my secret, so I put on a brave face. I even laughed along with some of the jokes, because I was the person who laughs at everything. If I stopped laughing, I was worried they would start looking at me.

When I made the decision to transition, I knew I needed to protect myself from my employer. I started making a journal of all the hateful comments and jokes. If they found out my secret, I felt like they were going to find a legal way to fire me for it. If that happened, I was ready to take them down!

Feeling like my current office environment was never going to be a safe place for me to come out, I started the search to find the employer that I felt the most comfortable to come out with. Beyond dealing with hate at work, I felt some urgency as I could see my physical changes occurring at a more rapid pace than I expected.

I knew exactly where I wanted to work. This organization not only marketed themselves as a place for everyone, but they had several LGBTQIA+ employees, along with a female-dominated leadership team. I interviewed with them for four months. I felt like the hiring manager liked me and I had good interviews with a couple of their executives. It was *in the bag*, or so I thought. One day I received a call that they were going in a different direction. I remember crying that day, as I was devastated.

About three months later, I interviewed with an organization that wanted to hire me a few years previously. The interviews were easy for both sides, because we all knew it would be a good fit. When I was offered the job, I accepted. There was nothing that was necessarily LGBTQIA+ friendly about this organization, but they had a good reputation and during my final interview they said, "we are like a family," and then shared stories of how much like a family they were. Good families embrace each other for their authenticity, and I had a good feeling that was about to happen.

My Parents Meet the Real Me

I was making plans to come out in a few months, and I knew my parents needed to meet the real me. I wrote them the following letter:

Mom and Dad,

I know you both are struggling with the thought of me transitioning. I don't know how many physical changes you have noticed, but the truth is I have been on hormones for the last three months. I started them before I moved out and called it quits on my marriage, because it was one of the many steps I have taken to make sure this was the right move for me.

I know you think I'm rushing into this, but the truth is I have been strategic and methodical every step along the way.

As I mentioned, I am likely coming out in about three months. I would hate for that to be your first exposure to my true self. As I said, I know you are struggling, but I think it's important that you meet the woman I am.

I would like to invite you over for dinner this Saturday to get to know the real me.

I love you and want you to be part of my life!

They accepted the invitation, and insisted they bring dinner. They brought my favorite, Mexican food. I could practically see their nerves standing on end as I peeked out the window, but as I opened the door, those nerves started to go away. They gave me a hug, and we proceeded to have a nice dinner. It was mostly just a normal time, and then we said our goodbyes.

My Birthday

I wrote the following on my birthday:

Today is my birthday and I'm taking it back! I am in such a different place in every possible way than last year, especially internally.

Last year, I hated my real birthday! At the time, it was difficult because I had a day that was so much more special to me, but not a single person here knew about it because I didn't feel like I was in a place to tell anyone. The day I'm talking about is the day I referred to in previous posts as my Jenn birthday. My Jenn birthday refers to the day I created a Facebook account on April 14, 2021, and started my journey to understand myself for the first time. What I really wanted was to celebrate that with my people and it was difficult. I went into a dark place for a while. The only thing I focused on was creating a countdown to celebrate my Jenn Birthday. And then when it came and went, it was even more difficult.

This year is the opposite. I know who I am, and by acknowledging that I am a transgender woman and through some great therapy, living on my own being me when I can, among other things, I am in such a good place to acknowledge Jenn was really born March 29th! April 14th I will continue to celebrate, but I'll call it my Jenniversary! It is still important, but I realized Jenn was really born thirty-eight years ago, and that has given me peace.

Jenniversary

The next month was my Jenniversary. I wrote:

Today is my Jenniversary. It was exactly two years ago that I created my first social media account as Jenn. It was that day I decided on the name Jennifer Marie, uploaded a picture and began a journey that would change my life, more than I ever imagined. At the time, I had no idea exactly what any of it meant or how deep this was for me. I just knew from the age of four that I have wanted to present as a woman, as much as I possibly could, and every opportunity since I have done exactly that.

I have been doing a lot of reflection this week. I realized when I created social media accounts for Jenn, I was living online. Since I started living in real life (part-time for now), I have spent a lot less time online. Last year around this time, I was living online. I literally created a Jenn birthday countdown, because I couldn't be me and I was living through that. And I wasn't happy. This year my life is completely different. I'm out living my life in the real world as much as I can, and I'm so happy!

That week I was thinking about how I wanted this milestone to be special. I was walking through Target, and I saw it . . . the closest thing I had ever seen to Grandma's pink silk nightgown and robe. Suddenly, I was four years old all over again; I still remember it, and how it made me feel. That day, so long ago, was the day I knew I was different.

I just wouldn't figure out why until thirty-three years later.

https://www.jennspire.com/23-earlytransition-jenniversary

Chapter Nine

Jenn's Firsts

Now that I had figured out who I was, I started to experience a little bit of life as Jenn (mostly in special circumstances). I told my immediate family and a few friends; found a new employer; started on HRT; and moved out of the home I'd shared with my wife . . . now it was time to start experiencing life in the real world. That came with a *lot* of firsts.

Big Day of Firsts

After a day of errands in boy mode, it was time to get ready. As I applied my makeup, I really took my time because I was going out into the public eye, and not just the gay bars. I decided recently that I needed to be out and about, and not just in the safe LGBTQIA+ spaces. After I was made up and dressed, I left for Jenn's first pedicure.

When I arrived at the nail salon for my first pedicure as my true self, I got out of my car and the wind was blowing my wig hair *everywhere*! I am sure anyone who saw me was laughing, because I couldn't keep it out of my face. I walked into the nail salon—the ambience and design of this place screamed *luxury*—and everyone stared at me, but I did not care. I just kept smiling. This was already a vastly different experience from my first pedicure over a year and a half before, but it mostly had to do with me.

You see the first time, I entered the salon feeling like a man. I was shaking, never removed my mask, and struggled to relax. *This* time, I entered a much fancier, more crowded salon as a confident woman, and I was relaxed. I did not care what people thought of me. I did notice that there were men getting pedicures which I thought was great, too. Not only was I relaxed being the real me, but I realized how safe of an environment it was for men, too.

After I told the woman at the front desk I had an appointment for a gel pedicure, she pointed me to the table with all the swatches of colors. I'm sure it will come as no surprise to you that I picked a light shade of pink.

I was then pointed in the direction of a footbath that was ready for me. I took off my shoes, rolled up my pants, and dipped my feet into the relaxing warm water. When my technician arrived, she handed me a remote, because the chair I was sitting in was a massage chair. I let that chair massage my back and shoulders the entire time she was making my feet all pretty. When the gel polish was all dry on my toes, I reluctantly turned off the massage chair, put on my strappy heels, and paid. I was windblown by the time I reached the car. After a couple selfies, beaming with happiness, it was off to Sephora for my first-ever makeup lesson.

I pulled up and parked a couple stores away from Sephora. I was eager to get to my lesson, but I was still twenty minutes early, so I walked up the street until I came to a boutique and walked in. I was greeted by two employees who asked if I was shopping for anything in particular. It was a cute store, and there was an adorable pink flowy dress that caught my eye; another day I might have considered it, but I was saving my money for my makeup lesson and the makeup I wanted to buy.

Walking a couple of doors down from that store, I encountered a woman who told me she loved my shoes. I was beaming as I walked into Sephora!

At check-in, the technician told me I could sit down while she was cleaning up. After I had taken a couple before selfies, and she had everything clean, I showed her the makeup I currently used, and she told me which ones seemed to be working really well for me. She also had some recommendations for new products I should try.

The entire makeup lesson was a great experience. She showed me techniques on how to apply various makeup and different products I had never used before. That day I was introduced to concealer and bronzer, and they became a regular part of my makeup routine. I loved having someone else apply makeup on my face for the first time since I stopped dressing up for Halloween. She was never pushy about products, but told me what she used. I told her which products I wanted, and she rang me up. Then, I was off to have dinner with my friend Ash to celebrate this special day of firsts.

Ash and I decided to have dinner at a local salad place. We talked about everything and used the words *trans* and *girls like us* so many times, but not a single person gave us a look. Chatting long after we had finished eating, Ash offered to show me her office and bridal showroom, as she was a wedding dress designer. All of the wedding dresses were beautiful, and I pictured myself wearing several! After the tour, we moved our conversation to the couch in the lobby. We chatted for about two more hours, and then decided to call it a night. I told her, "It's great having local friends who are so similar to me."

https://www.jennspire.com/24-jennsfirsts-bigdayoffirsts

Expectations

A couple months after I moved out, I was feeling less like me. I felt less estrogen in my body, and it increased my dysphoria. One day, I was on my computer and I noticed something: I had a message from my doctor that said I could increase my dosage of estradiol. I was ecstatic! I knew this would be good, but I never imagined to what extent. After I increased the dosage, I wrote:

I have felt more like myself this week than ever! I have more feminine feelings and emotions and I can't stop smiling. It has also made me dislike anything that feels fake in my life. I have started to fall in love with the woman I am, and I'm happier for it. I am ready to be done with the wig, so I started looking up cute short women's hairstyles online. I have been growing my hair out for a few weeks now, and I started playing with it. I got out the diffuser attachment for my blow dryer and afterwards I loved the woman I saw staring back at me. No makeup. Just me.

I have done a lot of reflecting this week. When I started this journey, I had so many expectations for what I wanted, and what my life would look like. I could name several surgeries I wanted, and over time I have reduced the number to only a couple, and other than that, I'll let the natural progression with hormones take their course and then see where I am.

Also, when I started my physical transition, I thought I would feel like a completely different person. I think I wanted an escape from who I was and to start over. I have since fallen in love with the woman I am, and my outlook has changed. It's so much more positive, but I'm still the same person who loves golf, tennis, fishing, drinking beer, and watching sports and I love it. Now don't get me wrong, things have changed. In addition to feeling everything deeper, I can finally express my love of the feminine. The way I have decorated my home has a feminine touch. Everything from pictures to pillows to designing my kid's rooms, it's all Jenn.

My expectations have been shattered, and now I'm just living my life and enjoying the ride. When I began my transition, I was dying to reach the end and just come out. I have finally taken the advice my counselor gave me a few months back and several other trans women have given me, "Slow down, enjoy the ride, and enjoy every first because you only get to do this once." I'm taking that advice and I'm happy.

https://www.jennspire.com/25-jennsfirsts-expectations

First Time at Church

After I moved out, I was so happy with who I was, but something was still missing . . . my relationship with God was not where I needed it to be. A couple of months before I moved out, I had stopped attending church. I told my wife and kids I needed to get things done at home, but the truth is LGBTQIA+ hate was being preached almost every week. After I realized I was so happy with who I was, I couldn't take it anymore; my spirit was simply starved for a church community.

The month after I moved out, I started trying out new churches who would not only accept the real me, but would affirmingly embrace me. I tried a few different ones until I found the right church. I attended in guy mode for a few months until I was ready to attend as the real me.

May 28, 2023, was the first time I walked into church as the real me. I wore a floral dress, heels, a wig (to protect my identity), a little jewelry, and my new makeup. I was ready. Was I nervous? Not very, actually.

Every step I took—no matter how big—gave me more confidence for the next step. I walked in the church doors greeting others with, "Good morning," and proceeded to walk down the hall into the sanctuary to find a seat. No one stared. I mean, I got looks (as I do everywhere, because I'm a 6′ 2″ girl, even without heels on), but nothing negative.

I had forgotten about the part at the beginning after we sang our first song where we each take time to greet and introduce ourselves to those around us. Typically, I shake about three hands. That day, I had close to ten people shake my hand. They all said hello and many asked me my name, to which I replied, "Jenn." I also got a lot of compliments on my dress. The only time I stumbled was when someone asked if it was my first time at this church. I just said no. It was awkward for me, because it felt weird to say, "No, I usually come in guy mode."

After shaking hands, I could feel a huge smile coming on. Being embraced as my true self felt amazing! After the service, as I was walking out, one of the church staff members stopped me and said, "I love your dress."

"Thank you!" I exclaimed, and started smiling again.

After church, I met up with some of the LGBTQIA+ church members for lunch. I was the only trans person there, but it didn't matter. There were even a couple who were allies. Everyone was so nice, and so interested in me, and included me in the conversation. I stayed until just about everyone had left, as I was savoring this moment. Near the end, the older lady who came with her husband as allies said, "I don't know if this is politically correct, but you look fabulous!" It was so sweet, and the perfect end to a perfect day out.

I continued attending church as the real me on Sundays when I did not have the kids until I was ready to come out. It felt odd to present as my fake male self one week, and then my true female self the next week, but I knew my kids weren't ready yet, and I felt it was important to be the real me as much as possible.

https://www.jennspire.com/26-jennsfirsts-firsttimeatchurch

A Surprising Day

June 3, 2023, was a weird but awesome day. I woke up with my daughter next to me, as she had snuck into my bed in the night. She was so freaking cute with that big smile on her face, cuddled up to me. A little later, she got out of bed and then came back in a few minutes to get me up. She did not even notice or care that I had ruffles on my black pj shorts and top. She noticed my painted toenails and said, "Your toes are painted like a girl's," and giggled. I said "Yeah, I like them. Aren't they pretty?" She agreed, and that was that. My son did not comment on my pjs or toenails all morning.

After the kids were ready, we headed to the local theme park for a fun day with some friends. My friend's brother and his husband bumped into us later in the day. I never expected to see them there, but I was thrilled and had this urge to come out to them if I got my moment. The first thing I did when they arrived, I told them both, "Happy Pride!" and received no response. I was not sure if they did not hear me, or if they thought it was weird that his brother's straight friend was saying it.

Later, I was chatting with them while the kids were on a train ride. I asked them if they typically go to Pride, and that I was headed there myself the following weekend. We had a nice little conversation about it.

When the kids were on the next ride, we somehow got to talking about drag bans and we both expressed our opposing thoughts on that and other LGBTQIA+ issues. We had a respectful, but passionate conversation. I am pro drag and if parents don't want their kids to see it, then don't bring them. I have not introduced my kids to drag, and may not until they are older, but that is my choice.

Later that day, when both my friends were away with all the kids, I told my friend's brother, "I haven't told your brother yet, but I will soon. I'm the *T*."

He knew exactly what I meant, and said he had friends who are trans men, but several of them wish they had never transitioned because in his words, they are "just gay." I felt surprised by this comment, and a little deflated.

Before I go any further, I want to explain something briefly, because many people in my life have had trouble understanding this, and it is very key in understanding transgender people. Transgender people are not necessarily gay. Transgender people can be heterosexual, homosexual, bisexual, or asexual. Transgender has to do with gender identity (who you are inside) while gay has to do with sexuality (whom you are attracted to).

He went on to say that his friends wished they had done therapy beforehand so they could have figured it out (that it had to do with sexuality, and not gender).

"I have done therapy for over a year," I replied, doing my best to remain even-keeled. "I know who I am, and I confirmed it even more after I started on hormones. After a couple of weeks on HRT, I finally felt right in my own body."

I'm not sure whether he felt I was getting defensive, or if he wanted to defuse the situation because his remark was off-putting for me to hear. And I don't think he intended it to be received in that manner; I think he was just stating what he knew about the trans community. Again, *gay* is not the same as *trans*, and just because you're part of the larger LGBTQIA+ community doesn't mean you are thoroughly familiar with all the other "letters" represented besides your own. Regardless, he said he was happy for me, and appreciated me sharing with him.

This conversation brought up a couple things for me. One, I have talked to a lot of people and done a lot of research. The percentage of people who detransition is extremely low, and the percentage of those people who regret ever beginning transition is even lower. He, like many people do, took a couple of cases and applied it to the entire group.

The other thing that conversation brought up for me was the importance of full self-exploration and therapy. Getting help to work though one's past, and what is going on internally, is extremely important. Each person is different as to how many sessions that entails. My experience was that after about a year of therapy, I was in a very good place to know what I wanted, what I needed and what it all meant for me.

Later, as we were heading out, we were all saying goodbye and he hugged me for the first time ever—a long, strong hug—and whispered in my ear, "You know, you and I may be on the opposite sides of some political issues, but I respect you and I am always here to support you." It took everything to keep from tearing up. It meant the world.

That night on the way home from the theme park, the strangest, greatest thing happened. Out of the blue, my daughter said, "I love you, but I want you to be our Mommy. Mommies are the best!"

"No, Daddies are the best," my son replied.

I asked them each why, and they just thought they were right, because as both said respectively, "They are the most fun."

"I need you guys to know something so please listen," I said carefully. "Whether I am your Mommy or your Daddy, we will always have fun. I'll always love you, be there for you, and take care of you. No matter if I'm a Mommy or Daddy, I'm still the same person doing all those things. So does it really matter if I am a Mommy or a Daddy?"

They thought about it for a minute. "No it doesn't," they both agreed.

First Pride Weekend

My first Pride weekend started off with Kira and Josie, two of my friends from Instagram, arriving at my place. Instead of going out to dinner the first night, we sat there just talking until 2:00 a.m. We already knew each other from chatting online, so we were able to go deep quickly, but connecting in person is very different and much more powerful.

Saturday, we slept in, got up and got ready while we talked more. We arrived at Pridefest in the middle of the afternoon. Walking down the street on the way to the festival, I immediately felt welcome and when I walked in the gate, I felt at home. With all the hateful people and legislation, this was not only a safe space, but one where I was embraced. I wore a dress that was designed to look like the trans flag, and I got so many compliments on it. There were a few different times people wanted their picture taken with us. This kind of acceptance made me feel warm inside.

I got to meet up with so many of my new friends at Pride. After we walked around Pridefest for six hours, watching drag on the main stage and more, we went back to get ready for the night. I wore my longer wig, skinny jeans, and a black top. We headed out for a great Pride night where we watched a bit more drag, talked to some older trans women, caught up with another friend, and danced a ton. It was another fun night!

Sunday, we slept in and got ready for brunch. Our server was so nice to us. We chatted, ate our delicious food, and then walked to our cars.

Kira had to leave because she had a long drive home. Josie was not feeling well, so she came back to my place to lie down for a bit. I could tell it was way more than just a headache. She was wrapped up in the weekend, thinking about everything. I had been there. I knew exactly what that was like. We got to talking, and I found out we are very similar in how we have experienced our gender, how our future is looking, and the challenges we were going to face. It was such an important conversation.

One of the things she said was she is proud to be a *trans* woman and not a woman. She said she never would want to take away from the cis woman's journey in that way.

This is not an uncommon feeling for many trans women. We recognize that we have not been through many of the same things in our journey and none of us want to take away from the cis woman's journey, but we don't want to be excluded from the circle, either.

Each of us has different feelings about how they identify. There are many transgender people who use they/them pronouns in place of or in combination with their other pronouns, while others of us do not want to feel "othered" in any way, so we use binary pronouns, like she/her.

That day it came full circle for me, because one of my favorite things I took away when I came out to my cousin was when she told me, "You're like a butterfly. God creates it to live one certain way as a caterpillar for a good portion of its life, and then it transforms and becomes something really beautiful."

I think everyone's different, but in my case, I think this is exactly how I was created. I also think when it comes to me it was very intentional, so I can help change the narrative by showing LGBTQIA+ people God's unconditional love—particularly those who have been shunned by the church. And I believe I was also created to show everyone that we are here just living our lives and we are nothing to be feared. The statistic I had heard was 70 percent of people do not think they know a trans person. I was going to change that statistic, one person at a time.

https://www.jennspire.com/27-jennsfirsts-firstprideweekend

Telling 100 People

After I decided to come out, I knew I wanted and needed to tell people—and not just because I like sharing my innermost personal secret with others.

There were several reasons, actually, but the biggest one was that my job was public-facing (I was one of the most community-involved people in our organization), and I knew that when I came out, the gossip would spread like wildfire. I wanted to get in front of it to control the message. I also wanted to show as many people in my life as possible that they were important enough for me to share this secret with.

I was very strategic about the people I told. I created a list (yes, *a list* lol—don't worry, a lot of people have laughed at me about it) of people I wanted to tell. It was not necessarily about whether I thought they would agree with me; it was about whether I could trust that they could keep it just between us. This created better relationships with most of those people. Many of them opened up and told me something that they were dealing with and many times it was about a trans or nonbinary family member that I did not know about.

Each conversation was a little bit different. Some were thirty minutes and some were three hours. Each time I shared it, something always surprised me about how they responded. Some challenged me and asked me extremely hard questions. I loved that, because I was able to answer every one. I loved those hard conversations with religious conservative people, because they created teaching moments. I loved every conversation.

There were several common elements in these conversations:

- I began every conversation with, "I am about to tell you something personal about me. If it gets out, it could ruin my life, so please do not share this with anyone else."
- I also said, "I'm the easiest person to talk to about this. Unlike many people like me, you can't offend me because this is about teaching and understanding."
- "You may have questions, as have many I have shared this with, so feel free to ask at any time or after I am done sharing."
- Then, I explained that I was transgender, and went into telling them my story. I shortened it or lengthened it, depending on the person and how much time we had.
- I explained that if I was gay, I just wouldn't tell many people, but this is outward, and you all are about to see me change more than ever. I made sure to include, "Just know I'm the same me."
- Finally, I would ask: "Do you know anyone else whom I should share with, someone who would be able to keep it to themselves?"

Most of the people I talked to had never had an opportunity to talk to someone like me, and if they had, they felt there were questions that they were always too afraid to ask. I told people any question that they asked out of respect or open curiosity, I would love to answer. It was very important to me to answer all these questions, so they would have a better understanding of me and my amazing transgender community.

As I was telling people, I realized I was creating an army of allies who knew my story and could defend me, if they felt compelled to do so. It was also freeing. Every day of my life I woke up with this big secret that I could not tell anyone. I felt like I was always hiding. When I started sharing, and more and more people knew, a huge weight began to be lifted off my shoulders.

Here are a few of my favorite moments:

> One fellow board member's response: "I will keep my mouth closed until you are ready, and then I won't." It made me feel good, because that was his way of saying, "I have your back, and I will not be quiet about that."

> My pastor's response: "It is a privilege for you to share your journey with me. How happy are you?!?! I am behind you and the church is behind you. You will always be welcome here and embraced as your true self." I wasn't presenting as Jenn when we met, so after, when she sent me a beautiful note thanking me for allowing her to witness God's work in my life, I sent her a picture of me. This was her beautiful response: "Jenn, you look incredible! So much joy and light. Congratulations!! I can't wait to see what the future has in store for you."

I was ready to tell the leader of our Rotary Club. The day before I told him, I learned that he grew up Catholic and his mom was a nun for part of her life.

The day arrived, and my heart started to pound in my chest, especially after what I had learned. I told him, "I am getting divorced, and it is because I am in the LGBTQIA+ spectrum and I know it's always kind of seemed like it's a 'don't ask don't tell' policy in our club, but that's not possible with me—because I am trans and proud of it, and hopefully coming out in about three months."

The second I told him this . . . he smiled and gave me a high five! It was the perfect gesture to let me know to *keep going, and I support you*. I started smiling and continued telling him everything, way more than I intended to. He was supportive of all of it and wanted to know my plan and how he could help.

I explained all the steps of getting a job with an accepting employer, proving I'm a great parent on my own, and then coming out hopefully in about three months. I told him about my coming-out speech. He told me, "Take out the part about the board meeting to discuss whether we want you to remain on the board. I need you here. You are invaluable to this club. And if anyone wants to quit our club because of it, I will be thrilled, because we don't want that hate here. It's not what Rotary stands for, and we will support you."

I almost broke down, it was such a relief and a blessing to hear those words!

Then he said, "If you would feel comfortable, I would love for you to give your speech in front of the club. The true emotion and honesty will resonate well with people." That day, I decided when I was ready, I would give the speech live in front of the club. I was nervous, but this seemed like the perfect way to come out.

"I can tell how much careful planning you have been doing," he continued. "It's so methodical, but I'm so sorry that people aren't accepting, and you have to do that. One day, you shouldn't have to do much of that anymore." That made me so happy. It was the warmest response I could have imagined.

I have a friend named Bill, who is also a mentor. Bill is a great guy, but one thing to know about Bill is he will tell you exactly what he thinks. He is also a devout Christian. With Bill being a mentor and a highly respected member of my business community, I knew I needed to tell him. I was a little nervous to tell him because I knew he wouldn't hold anything back.

The day before I had scheduled to tell him, the most amazing thing happened. I went to an LGBTQIA+ business event that day for the first time. I was in guy mode, but had Jenn on my name tag. I showed up and as soon as I walked in the door, the leader, who is my friend, approached me.

"Guess who's here?" she asked with enthusiasm.

"Who?" I replied, quickly scanning the room.

"Bill!"

My heart was so happy! A little later I spotted him. I walked up to him and said, "So I can't go anywhere without running into you?" He laughed and hugged me.

Pointing to my name tag, I said, "Here's the reason I've been wanting to talk to you."

Peering down to read it, he said, "Jenn . . . okay, good for you. I'm here as an ally, because my son recently told me he is gay. I told him, 'I love you,' and I did not say 'despite' or 'anyway.' He's my kid, and I just love him."

The next day, I met with Bill as originally planned. We mostly talked about business, but we did touch on what happened the previous night. The main thing he said to me was this: "I'm proud of you. It takes a lot of courage to do what you're doing. God doesn't make mistakes, and you're just being who you were meant to be. Everyone deserves to be happy, and I'm glad you've found a way to be happy."

Hearing those words, I got emotional. I told him that he was the sixty-seventh person I have had a conversation like this with, and after giving me crap for him being further down the list, he offered to prepare some of the more difficult people I still had to tell, so things will be better received. I was nervous about telling Bill, but in the end he became one of my strongest supporters.

To All of the People Who Are Scared to Share Their Authentic Self: *You never know how someone will accept your truth until you give them that chance to know your truth and respond.*

Roller Coaster Weekend

July 8th, 2023, I had a couple of really great conversations about coming out. One of my business friends and I became closer by sharing my truth with her. She wanted to get to know the real me;

we started messaging each other for the first time. She invited me to a party, and while I would have loved to attend, the date she mentioned was over a weekend that I had the kids. I had to decline the invitation, but told her I would still love to get together or be included the next time.

This was not the first, nor the last time, something like this has happened.

People could see my internal joy; it was shining outwardly, and I think they wanted to be part of it by getting to know the real me. I love sharing it with anyone, being able to bring joy to this world.

After work that same day, I had another incredible evening. I hurried home and got ready in about thirty minutes. My amazing photographer had gotten her own studio, so she was having an open house. A trans man and his partners were going to be there. A mutual friend had introduced us online, and we had talked a bit about how we are looking forward to meeting in person at the open house.

I did not know anyone but the photographer, so I was a little awkward until he showed up with his partners. When they arrived, I quickly came to life. I immediately loved them all. We talked for hours about everything—long after all the guests were gone, and the photographer was hanging out with us a bit. It was a great evening . . . but it wasn't over yet.

After we said our goodbyes, I took a couple more selfies and walked out the door. I called my sister, who was heading to a hotel a few minutes away from my location. She invited me to join her, her boyfriend, and another couple they are friends with. We met up and had a great time having a drink on the patio of this swanky hotel. Everyone was incredibly nice to me, treating me like one of the girls. It was an amazing feeling! My sister and I had grown really close, maybe closer than we had ever been. I know I felt that way, because I literally had no secrets from her anymore.

Saturday morning . . . I had two plans I was really excited about. First, I got cute and met up with a cis woman. One of the things my counselor told me in the final session I had with her that really stuck with me was, "Make sure you surround yourself with cis friends, too. If you only hang out with trans people, your life will revolve around trans, which can increase dysphoria." Therefore, I was trying to make more cis girlfriends.

We met up at a coffee shop downtown. I immediately knew we were going to be good friends. She had great energy and she's a hugger! We had some good coffee and even better conversation. We even made plans for her to go with me in a couple weeks to get my ears pierced for the first time!

Then I was off to meet my cousin for the first time as my true self and get pedicures together. The pedicures were wonderful and relaxing, but our conversations were the best part.

As I was driving home from the pedicure, I started to get inside my head. I had recently tiptoed into online dating. I was chatting with a couple guys, one of whom I was really starting to like. We talked for a few days. I had been hinting at him—subtly at first, then a little more directly—about a date, hoping he would ask me.

As time progressed, I kept getting more anxious, because I had never been on this side of the asking and I refused to ask him. I wanted to be pursued, and for *him* to ask *me* on a date. After the pedicure, I was alone with my thoughts and my hormones started taking over. I couldn't shake this thought of, "Just ask me out. This is driving me crazy waiting. Does he really like me? Would he actually date me?" etc. I got home, and it got even worse. I was spiraling!

I finally took a nap, ate a very late lunch, had a couple drinks, watched one of my girly rom coms on Netflix, and I felt a whole lot better and in control of my thoughts and feelings. Then I started journaling until I called it a night.

My alarm went off early Sunday morning. I was not normally a morning person, but a friend introduced me to this trans woman she's friends with and she likes to run in the morning, so we made plans to walk together. We met up at 7:00 a.m. (Yes, it was early for me on a weekend) and walked several miles together. She was a couple months behind me on HRT, but she was doing things very differently. She was fully out and proud, wore trans socks, had a trans flag sticker on her car, etc. Me . . . I was transitioning "under the radar."

We talked the entire time. We both had deep respect for how the other one was transitioning. It was a really nice time until we ran into someone I knew!

We were walking along and then a group ran by us in the other direction. One of the girls called out to my friend, as they used to be good friends. As they were talking, I glanced over and saw someone that I knew through my business life! I immediately looked away and stared at my phone in the other direction. I was anxious the entire way back that we would run into them again.

I started walking faster and faster. My heart was pounding. "Did he recognize me?" (Still to this day I do not know the answer to that.) Afterward, we were in the parking lot, and I heard that same group approaching, so I jumped in my car and ducked. I waited for them to pass, and hurried out of there.

I drove straight home, took a shower, and got dressed for church. As I had done the other times, I walked into church confidently, smiling ear to ear. I greeted the staff that I knew and made my way to sit with one of my friends, who was saving a seat for me. I had never met his husband, so we chatted a bit and then the songs started. I felt so at home in my church. Again, after the first song we shook hands, and it went amazing . . . as it always did.

After the service, some of our other LGBTQIA+ friends came by while we were chatting. They were meeting up to discuss leadership stuff for our upcoming LGBTQIA+ events. I said goodbye as I had plans to meet up with another cis girl from the friendship side of the dating app.

I apologized for being a few minutes late to lunch, and we chatted for hours. After I was done eating, I ordered a beer, so we could chat longer. It turned out she was in my pickleball league, so we talked a little bit about that, but mostly we talked about other things. She identified as Queer. Believe it or not, I have terrible gaydar, so we laughed about that, talked about how she's new to town within the last year, and the conversation went on from there. Being Sunday, we both had things to do to get ready for the week, so after almost three hours of conversation, we hugged and parted ways.

I got home, put on my short shorts and matching athletic top and started cleaning and doing laundry. Another fantastic weekend. This one had some ups and downs, but that's how life is. I was living it and I wouldn't have it any other way.

https://www.jennspire.com/28-jennsfirsts-rollercoasterweekend

Getting My Ears Pierced

The day finally arrived to get my ears pierced. I had wanted to do this for a long time, so I was excited. I had heard stories of infection and the holes not being even, so I made an appointment with a piercing shop.

My friend met me at the shop. As I waited for her to arrive, I picked out the studs I liked. I really wanted something prettier, like the cubic zirconium ones, as they looked like diamonds, but as I was still in guy mode most of the time, so I chose some small grayish blue ones that I liked. When my friend arrived, she agreed with my selection.

It was time for me to go back into the room. I was a little nervous, but mostly excited. The first one did not hurt a bit, but the second one was painful. My friend was recording the whole thing. In the video you can see this "big ouch" face I made. After the studs were installed, it was totally worth it.

My friend and I had a drink afterward and then parted ways.

https://www.jennspire.com/29-jennsfirsts-gettingmyearspierced

First Big Event

In August 2023, I attended my first big event. It was really large, and I was nervous. I was used to walking into a restaurant and having all eyes on me, but this was a whole new level of that, and bathrooms with other women always made me nervous—even though, to date, I'd not had a negative encounter in that respect. No one ever told me I didn't belong in there. Attending an event this large, however, practically guaranteed there would be lines for the restroom—and the thought of standing in a line like that also brought my anxiety to a whole new level.

The event was an Ed Sheeran concert. After I calmed myself down enough to step out of my car, I proceeded toward the stadium alone (a new friend was meeting me there), walking through rows of people seated in chairs tailgating before the concert. I could feel every one of them looking at me and I could see it, too. I just smiled, because I had never been happier, and I just owned it. I owned the day.

After I was inside, I got looks, but not a single one bothered me. The times I went to the restroom, not a single incident occurred. And Ed Sheeran . . . he put on a spectacular show!

https://www.jennspire.com/30-jennsfirsts-firstbigevent

Queer Stories

I had been asked weeks previously if I wanted to share my story at an event my church created called Queer Stories. It was open to the entire community, and a few people would be sharing their stories. The goal was to not only inspire, but encourage other LGBTQIA+ people to try our church. I jumped at the opportunity.

I shared my story with about sixty other awesome LGBTQIA+ people, mostly associated with my church. It was phenomenal! After I shared a shortened version of the story of my journey, I gave the same speech I had planned to give less than two months later and the audience loved it!

I had thirteen people, including my cousin and her family, show up to support me and everyone in the room was also awesome and supportive. In my previous life, I was nervous and shaking about public speaking, but the day I spoke at Queer Stories, I was so calm and confident. I was being me, and I was just happy.

I was so excited I could share this experience with my cousin and her family and some of my other friends. I had the most amazing conversation with my cousin's son afterward about how he had been questioning where he fits into the gender spectrum; I just encouraged him. "You will find out where you belong," I explained. "Take your time, don't rush it, and remember—just because you find a place to land, don't get stuck. The gender spectrum is huge, and it doesn't mean that's where you stay. About this time last year, I thought I was dual gender, and now my life is in a completely different place, and I'm so much happier."

Romance

I had been on HRT for months and was living privately as a proud transgender woman. I was sitting on my couch one day watching a teen rom com on Netflix and it felt different—*good* different.

You see, I had always been what I referred to as a hopeless romantic. I used to sit watching rom-coms and just smile on the inside, because they made me happy. I had always loved watching love, whether it was on the screen or in real life. I had always cheered for true love.

I thought I wanted to be that way doing romantic things for the girls I was with, but in truth, I was actually terrible at it. I remember constantly thinking, "Why can't I be like that? I love when they do it in the movies." I would fail constantly to have any motivation to do random, sweet, romantic things. It took me many years to finally realize why.

I realized that day I have always wanted to be the *girl* having someone do romantic things for her . . . because I am a girl who loves those things. I was literally sitting there watching the mushy parts and clutching my chest naturally and I thought to myself, "I wouldn't want it any other way."

Harry

I have previously mentioned the person I am about to tell you about. We met on Instagram, and we connected instantly. This person identified as transgender, but would never transition. Her name was Meghan (No, not the same Meghan who organized the girls' weekends). I have talked to a lot of people on social media, but no one ever understood me as well as Meghan did. Not only did she know me better than I knew myself at times, but she also challenged me to become a better, healthier version of myself.

You see, as I was moving out—and for a while after—I was eating almost solely frozen foods, staying up late, never exercising, and taking overall terrible care of myself. She challenged all of these things; I accepted the challenge, and felt better because of it. We got to know each other so well, and I trusted them so much, that things began to shift for me.

As our conversations progressed, I hinted that I would like them to take me on a date with them in guy mode. For months, I had wanted to go on a date with a guy. I wasn't sure if it was just that going on a date with a man would make me feel more feminine, but I expected it was more than that. You see, as I finally admitted to myself that I was transgender, I started looking at my wife differently. I started looking at her like an equal, or at least how I wanted to look.

Here's an example: I was always a "boob guy," but I started looking at her and thinking *I want breasts,* and they became less enticing. I realized the world tells men to be "boob guys," so I was just following my training my entire life.

When I told Counselor #4 about this shift, she explained it perfectly. "You said when you were growing up, it was easier to make friends with girls," she said. "And that most years of middle school and after, you had a girlfriend. Maybe you wanted to be so close to girls, watching what they wore and how they behaved, that proximity made you think you were attracted to them."

Back to my friend . . . I asked them to take me on a date because I wanted to experience it with someone I felt safe with. As our conversations continued, I started calling him Harry and we rarely talked about Meghan. He didn't want to think about being Meghan, because he said that was never going to make him happy, and he knew I wanted Harry. As we started talking as Harry and Jenn, we started talking on the phone daily, sometimes for hours.

When I went to Asheville for my second girls' weekend, my layover on my way home happened to be in his city. I did not have but a couple hours there, but Harry bought a plane ticket that he would later cancel just to get through airport security to come see me. I did not feel confident traveling in girl mode yet, so I was in guy mode. He did not care. I sat down at the airport restaurant with a glass of chardonnay while I waited for him to join me. When he walked in, I didn't care that I was in guy mode, we had a long hug and then sat down in the booth together. He had his hand on my leg the entire time, even while we were eating.

After lunch was done, he paid and we walked hand-in-hand to the exit. Just before we arrived at the exit, we had a long hug. He said, "I really want to kiss you, and I don't care who sees."

"I don't want my first kiss to be in guy mode," I replied, and then I kissed him on the cheek.

After our lunch date, we continued to talk on the phone daily. One day when we were on the phone, Harry said, "I don't want this to scare you, but the way you are talking about how you feel about me, I think you are in love with me."

Oh Harry, there is no way I am in love with you, I thought. And then I did what I always do: I researched and reflected.

I found an article on OprahDaily.com[5] and according to them, here are the signs:

- You want to share your world with them. ✔
- They're always in your thoughts. ✔
- You feel like a teenager again. (Happy, giddy, energetic, euphoric and youthful.) ✔✔✔✔
- They become a priority and you make time for them. ✔
- You crave them, find their quirks attractive and they make you feel better about yourself. (I even liked when he would go on rants about random things in his Italian voice.) ✔✔✔
- You're ignoring other attractive people. ✔
- You feel the love everywhere, seeing everything in a new light. ✔
- Their traits become your traits. ✔

The list in the article goes on, but as I was reading this and checking off the imaginary boxes, I started crying. I knew I was in love with Harry, but I couldn't be . . .

You see, Harry and I are slightly over twenty years apart. I realized I didn't want just the last twenty or so years of Harry's life. I wanted *the entire thing*. I wanted to grow old with him, and not just watch him grow old and start over or be alone after he is gone. We both wished there was a time machine that he could get in and come find me.

---

5. King, Stephanie L. 2024, "Not Sure if You're Falling in Love? Here's Exactly How to Know." Oprah Daily, April 23, 2024, https://www.oprahdaily.com/life/relationships-love/a29267937/how-to-know-falling-in-love/.

The even bigger thing that I could never get past was breaking up a family. Harry was unhappily married with children that weren't much younger than me. If he left his wife, not only was he going to lose his wife, but he would also lose his children. He said he would give it all up for me. I could not be the reason for that to happen.

Every single person who knew about my feelings for Harry thought I was crazy. Whether they told me or not, it was obvious.

In the end, Harry was my first love as my true self. He went out of his way to not only make me feel special, but feel safe and comfortable. I knew in my heart it would come again with the right person, but I was in no hurry.

https://www.jennspire.com/31-jennsfirsts-harry

Online Dating

After my relationship with Harry ended, I was ready to find my person, so I joined the world of online dating. I had done this a little bit in college, but being on the female side, this was totally different.

I started on the friend side of the app and made friends with some cis women whom I am still friends with to this day. After I felt comfortable there, I opened my profile up to being interested in both men and women. I was not sure whether I was still interested in women, but I was curious and open to find out.

There were not many women who liked my profile, and none ever continued chatting after they learned about me, but the number of men who did was overwhelming! For a few months, I paid for a premium plan, so instead of just liking profiles and getting notified if we matched, I weeded through the hundreds of men who liked my profile. I learned that most men just look at your cover picture and swipe right or left. I know this because the first thing on my profile was the transgender flag, and throughout my profile I said a couple times that I was a proud transgender woman. Many men would delete the match while others responded. If they responded, I sent the following response:

I liked your profile, so we matched. In case you didn't read mine, I'm a proud Christian transgender woman with school-age kids. If you're still interested, I look forward to getting to know each other. If not, I wish you the best! 🖤

Most would delete my profile after that. Others would respond, "Sorry, I'm looking for a woman." I didn't even respond to the insult. There were several others who said they were happy for me and continued to talk, saying they were accepting. Some would just ghost me, while others chatted with me for a while. One guy even asked me on a date, to which I accepted, as we had chatted a good bit.

We met up for a sushi lunch date. He was almost as tall as me, which I really liked, but this was never a requirement. The sushi was great and our time was fine. At the end of the date, we walked out of the restaurant and then he kissed me again and again, long and hard, and then we said goodbye.

I realized then I liked kissing men, but I wanted more from him. I realized that for the entire date, I was carrying the entire conversation; not only was I doing all of the talking, but he also never asked me a single question. It was exhausting, but he was such a nice guy and treated me exactly as the woman I am. I said *yes* to a second date, hoping he would open up and it would be a two-way conversation. Unfortunately, that never happened. He kissed me again. It felt forced, and I was still not into it.

When I got home, I reflected overnight and made the decision to text him.

> *I'm not the girl who is going to ghost guys or lead them on. I had a good time last night as I have had chatting with you on both of our dates, but something is missing for me. It's just that spark. You really are the nicest guy, so much that I wish there was more there. I want to wish you all the best!*

He responded, and wished me all the best, too.

After that, I chatted with many other guys on the app, but they were all the same. They just wanted casual sex, or they were too worried about what other people thought to be seen with me. I refused to go over to someone's place, or let them come to mine, until we met in public. I was not that kind of girl, but even more, this was a matter of safety. If they were not willing to meet me in public first, then they would not get me. (I said this in a much nicer way to them.)

Some were persistent that they were trustworthy, while others were understanding. They all ended up ghosting me. After this happened five times in a row, I deleted my account.

I deserved better and thought, *Eventually I'll find my prince or princess, only time will tell.*

Chapter Ten

Almost Ready

Before I go any further, I need to tell you about my professional life.

I worked in a conservative field in an even more conservative customer-facing position, so I was very careful not to raise suspicions about me and waited to come out at work. Months before I came out publicly, I came out to our Director of HR, who was supportive. She said she had never had an employee who was going to transition, but we would figure this out together; she thought everyone would be supportive, and that how and when I wanted to come out to my team was completely up to me.

A couple weeks later, I was chatting with a few coworkers when one of them brought up how ridiculous it was that Target had been issued a cease and desist on all Pride items. The other three women all were outraged. The conversation continued in such a way that I felt like all of these people were going to accept my true self. I had planned on waiting until a little closer to my coming out date to talk to people at work, but these people had made it abundantly clear where they stood. Feeling confident that they would support me, I decided to tell them about me.

I called each one of them on the phone that night and told them. The first person I called, I asked her how she thought our boss's boss would respond. She said, "He'll be great. I mean he's supportive of her . . ." It was then that I learned one of these four women that I was calling that night was a lesbian herself. (They razzed me for weeks about the fact that I have the worst gaydar. I told you! LOL!)

Each one of these women, in fact, felt that our boss and boss's boss would both be supportive, so I told my immediate supervisor first. She said, "That's great! I just want you to be happy! You can do your job regardless, so I'm here to support you." It was an amazing feeling!

The next day I sent my boss's boss an email about getting together to meet privately in my office. I received a phone call shortly after. He said, "I already know, and I'm so happy for you! It has spread throughout the entire organization because people are so happy for you! Everything I have heard is positive. If anyone does not treat you well, I want you to come and talk to me." I was stunned! First, I was almost emotional, because I never anticipated that not only would people at my work *accept* me—but that they would be *excited* for me to be my true self. Icing on the cake!

I also got a little nervous that it would start to spread outside the organization, so I started taking steps to make sure I was ready to come out at any time.

I reached back out to the Director of HR and told her how everything had gone so well coming out with my team. I also told her about my concern that it would start to get outside the organization, which would force me to come fully out early. I asked that we go ahead and order a new name tag, desk name plate, and business cards. She said most of those things would be super easy, but she discovered there is a compliance issue that prohibits me from putting Jenn or Jennifer on my business cards when it is not my legal name, so I reached out to an attorney about starting that process.

Telling My Kids

This was one of the most difficult nights of my journey. It was another roller coaster! With a counselor and my ex sitting in the room, I told my eight- and six-year-old kids why I had been changing. I had been preparing them for months with small changes, reading them books about different types of people and families, and having subtle conversations.

As the night began, I read the book *Red* by Michael Hall. It is about a red crayon that is blue on the inside, but goes through a lot of challenges before he realizes he is blue. It is a beautiful book I read to my kids dozens of times. Like every other day we read this book, after we were done, I asked the kids what they liked about the book.

My daughter said what she always did when I asked her that question. "I like when he realizes he's blue and not red." My son was already thinking differently that night, and he gave me a completely different answer than usual: "I like that he always keeps trying."

"I also like when the other crayon asks him to try to draw an ocean anyway," he continued. He had said that about the ocean before, but never said anything about how he likes that he keeps trying, even though he can't color anything red.

Next, we read a fantastic book that the counselor had called *She's My Dad* by Sarah Savage. This beautifully written book is told from the child's perspective who tells about their male-to-female transgender father. As soon as the book was finished, my ex, visibly upset, asked who decided these books were a good idea.

To which the counselor pointed to her book and replied, "This book was my suggestion."

I pointed to *Red* and replied, "And this book was my idea."

Raising her voice, she stated that she would have really liked to have known in advance that this was going to happen.

"Okay," the counselor replied, and we moved on.

After reading *She's My Dad*, my son first remarked, "That is weird. Boys can't be girls."

"The parent in the book is not a boy," I replied.

"The parent was born a boy with boy parts," the counselor explained. "But on the inside, she feels like a girl, so she's making changes to match that on the outside."

My son just looked at me. "Dad, you have earrings."

"Yes, I do."

"Dad, are you the book?"

"Yes, I am like the *girl* in the book. I have been making changes to make my outside match my inside."

"But that doesn't make sense. You're a boy."

"No, I'm a girl on the inside, and I just look like a boy. I'm making changes to fix that."

"I don't like that," he said flatly. "I don't want you to change. I want you to be normal."

His mother interjected and agreed, telling my son she didn't like it, either.

Thankfully, the counselor validated both. "You each have a right to feel whatever way you want to," she explained. I agreed, and continued.

"I'm happier now than I ever have been," to add my feelings to the conversation. "I'm finally happy on the inside for the first time in my life."

My ex snarkily questioned that I have never been happy.

"Not inside with myself, "I told her. "I have never been happy or felt 'synchronized' on the inside and outside. Until now."

We all paused for a moment. I needed to catch my breath, and my ex was likely counting to ten.

"I knew I was different since before I was your age," I continued, now shifting my response to my children. "So you don't need to worry about this happening to you."

"Daddy is changing," said the counselor. "Mom, are you changing?"

My ex scoffed, and replied that she would never change because God made her this way.

"Mommy feels like a girl on the inside," the counselor continued, ignoring my ex's attitude. "So she's going to be a girl, but Daddy's feels like a girl on the inside, so Daddy is going to change to make the outside match that to be a girl."

"Mom and I have very different feelings about this," I explained to them. "But I also believe God made me in the way that I am going to be. And people have different thoughts and opinions about things. And that's okay."

My ex stated that we both have very different thoughts on this big issue, and that is why we are not going to be together. I agreed.

"Dad, these changes that are happening . . . Does it change anything about how you feel about your kids?" asked the counselor.

"No. No changes could ever change anything about how I feel about both of you," I said firmly.

The counselor continued. "Dad, what do you want the kids to call you? Can they still call you Dad?"

"Mom!" my daughter responded gleefully.

My ex insisted that they couldn't use any names like Mom, Mommy, Momma as *those are taken*!

"You both can call me whatever you want," I interrupted. "Even if you each choose to call me something different than the other. *You* get to choose. Mom doesn't get to decide that, and I am not going to decide that. That's *your choice*."

We got into some silly names like "toilet," but my point was made. And that sort of broke the tension that had been building within that conversation.

We also checked in multiple times with the kids during this conversation to see how they were feeling.

"I'm happy," my daughter replied.

This appeared to piss off my ex, as she asked why my daughter was so happy about this, in a way that felt much more like a statement than a question.

My daughter didn't reply.

"I don't like it," said my son. "I don't want you to change. I don't want to be confused. I want to know who you are."

To which the counselor and I assured him that these changes would continue to happen slowly. "You will continue to see me a lot, and you will always know who I am," I explained.

My son wanted other people to know who I am. "Then you can tell them, or not," we told him. "It's up to you."

Toward the latter part of the conversation, my son said something that was hard to hear.

"I am going to pray to God," he said. "I'm going to pray that he makes you a boy. God is magic and he can do anything."

I told him he could do whatever he wanted and that it was up to him.

At the end of the session, my son was still a little shaken up. My ex asked him if he wanted to come home with her.

"Or do you want to go see the new puppy?" I asked. In the end, he chose to go with me, and I was so grateful.

We continued to have great conversations the entire way home, talking about how some things—like growing my hair long—have happened so far, and has anything changed in our relationship as a result? Do I love you less?

"No . . ."

"You're right," I replied. "And nothing will ever change about how I feel about you." After a lot of conversation, we ended with the fact that he did not really like it, but he said we are good. I told him I loved him, and he said it in return.

We got home and he played with the puppy for a few minutes, which made him feel better. Then he played a racing game on this tablet, showing me how he plays. I watched him play the entire ten minutes until I had to take them back to their mother's house.

That connection appeared to help him even more to know that I am still the same. It was a roller coaster of a night, but the three of us made it to the end and got off the ride, with smiles on all our faces.

Kids Are the Cutest

Over the next several months, difficult conversations happened with both kids, but mostly with my son. One day they were okay with everything, and the next, they told me they wanted me to change back to a boy. I recognized this was all part of the process.

I want to share a journal entry that shows how quickly and how far my son had come during this period. I wrote this within a month of telling my kids:

I can't stop smiling again! My son just randomly told me, "It's okay if your voice changes. It should sound more like a girl. You also need to marry a boy so he can help you do things. You should grow out your hair and then you can marry a boy."

I asked him if this is what he wants. He said, "Yes, then we can be a family."

My daughter agreed and said he can play the game "Hands Down" with us.

I asked my son if I marry a boy, what are you going to call me. He said, "Mom."

Taking them back to their mother's house tonight, he told me, "When you marry a boy, you can sit there," and pointed to the passenger seat.

My kids are the cutest!

Barbie Movie

The Barbie movie had been out for months, and I was dying to see it. I asked a friend who had already seen it to join me for dinner and the movie. That night, I had a pre-dinner drink called Midwest Heatwave, partly because it was 100 degrees outside and partly because I just love rum and pineapple juice; given that this cocktail is also mixed with strawberry and jalapenos, I could not pass it up. After a nice hanger steak and vegetables, summer salad, molten chocolate cake, and sparkling wine, we were off to the movies.

As expected, the movie was fabulous. It was smart, funny, and cute, but I never imagined the effect it would have on me. As I watched the part where they show mother-daughter relationships . . . for the first time in my life, I got emotional about not having a girlhood and not having those mother-daughter moments. It was hard to think about moments lost, but I did as I always do: I focused on the positive.

I had a mother who met me where I was. She helped me dress up when various gender-bending opportunities came about. Even though she didn't know exactly what she was doing at the time, in her own way, she was supporting me. She also showed me a lot of love, and showed me *how* to love. So, in my own way, I had those moments with her.

I also got emotional at the end when Barbie is told about all the difficult things that women have to deal with in the real world. She is then given a choice . . . Does she go back to her simple easy "perfect" life, or does she go live in the real world with all of its flaws and imperfections? Barbie chooses to live her life in the real world, despite all the challenges that come with it.

That really hit home for me, and I started crying. The film hits hard on the societal expectations people put on women, especially those who are mothers. Women are also still fighting for equal pay in the workforce, and now they are fighting for their right for bodily autonomy. People who think that trans women don't have to deal with these issues are so wrong. While we do not experience some of the bodily changes (but many do, if we are on HRT), we experience many of the societal expectations, equal pay for trans women is even worse than cis women experience (Transgender women, who hold both a marginalized gender (e.g., woman) and gender identity (e.g. transgender), report the largest gap of all, earning approximately 60 cents for every dollar the typical U.S. worker earns[6].), and our rights to bodily autonomy are under

6. Human Rights Campaign, "The Wage Gap Among LGBTQ+ Workers in the United States," accessed July 11, 2024, https://www.hrc.org/resources/the-wage-gap-among-lgbtq-workers-in-the-united-states#:~:text=LGBTQ%2B%20Pay%20Gap%20by%20Gender,typical%20worker%20increased%20to%2013%25.

attack as legislators try to strip us of our right to gender affirming care. Even though I was going to have to deal with those challenges and more, there was no question about what I needed to do . . . like Barbie, I chose that life, because that is real. I said to myself, "Jenn is who I am, and it's all so close I can almost taste it."

https://www.jennspire.com/32-almostready-barbiemovie

It's Getting Real

About a month before I came out, something difficult happened. My boss suggested that I move away from the front of the office to the back, for my own safety once I came out. She allowed it to be my choice, however, so this was not a directive but merely a consideration for my comfort and safety.

I loved being close to the action and not feeling secluded, but it did not take me two seconds to think about it. Unfortunately, she was right—at least temporarily, I did not need an office near the front where certain hateful customers could be nasty to me once I fully presented as Jenn . . . especially if they already knew me from before. I knew it was going to be hard, because this was the first negative change I had to make.

I wrote the following:

The move was finalized yesterday. I like my new office and all I did was move offices, but this represents just the beginning of challenges coming my way because I'm being who I was meant to be. This is hard, but as one of my favorite people Glennon Doyle says, "We can do hard things!"

Fighting for My Plan

I already shared about how amazing the Rotary Club Board President's response was. To allow more time to prove myself at work and come out to my kids slowly, however, I pushed my coming-out date back several months.

What was the significance of coming out at a Rotary meeting? Rotary International is committed to diversity. In addition to allowing the LGBT+ Rotary Fellowship to be created in the past few years, which can be found at Rotarylgbt.org, Rotary strengthened it's DEI statement[7] saying:

> *At Rotary, we understand that cultivating a diverse, equitable, and inclusive culture is essential to realizing our vision of a world where people unite and take action to create lasting change.*
>
> *We value diversity and celebrate the contributions of people of all backgrounds, across age, ethnicity, race, color, disability, learning style, religion, faith, socioeconomic status, culture, marital status, languages spoken, sex, sexual orientation, and gender identity as well as differences in ideas, thoughts, values, and beliefs.*

7. Rotary International. "Diversity, Equity, and Inclusion." Rotary. 2019. https://www.rotary.org/en/about-rotary/diversity-equity-and-inclusion.

> *Recognizing that individuals from certain groups have historically experienced barriers to membership, participation, and leadership, we commit to advancing equity in all aspects of Rotary, including in our community partnerships, so that each person has the necessary access to resources, opportunities, networks, and support to thrive.*
>
> *We believe that all people hold visible and invisible qualities that inherently make them unique, and we strive to create an inclusive culture where each person knows they are valued and belong.*
>
> *In line with our value of integrity, we are committed to being honest and transparent about where we are in our DEI journey as an organization, and to continuing to learn and do better.*

The Rotary calendar ends after June, so by July, we had a new President. President #2 came from a generation that is generally slower at accepting different concepts. He was more conservative, but still a good person. I knew I needed to share with him my plans to come out during a Rotary Club meeting, but I also needed back-up.

In rare circumstances, I would bring along another person to support me during a coming-out conversation with another person. This would be one of those times. I brought my friend from Rotary Club who has a non-binary child.

By far, it was my most difficult conversation. He told me he did not understand what I was doing, but he supported me as a person and that would not change. He was against me coming out during a Rotary meeting, but agreed to leave it up to the board to decide.

He said we could discuss it at a closed board meeting, which was fine with me . . . but before that was scheduled, I needed to tell everyone individually. I told him I would get back to him after I had those conversations.

One-by-one, I told the people in the club. Of the hundred people I came out to, this group made up about twenty percent of that. The conversations with all of the board members went well; some asked hard questions, and some did not. They all were supportive of me, and none expressed concern regarding me giving my coming-out speech in front of the club.

After I had told the last person, I shared with President #2 that everyone knew.

The next month's board meeting lasted about two-and-a-half hours. Everyone was exhausted, and then President #2 mentioned that we had one more item to discuss that was not on the agenda. He proceeded to bring up my request to give my coming-out speech in front of the club. He stated strongly that he was completely against this. I recall him referring to it as a self-serving act that has no place in Rotary. The way that this was presented at the end of a meeting, after many members had already left, caught me off-guard. He then proceeded to open it up to the group.

Everyone was silent for a minute and then one of the members voiced their concern, and a couple more agreed. I was completely blindsided! The President was the only person who expressed any issue with this, and now several more did.

I could see this opportunity to come out in front of the club slipping away, and tears started to well up in my eyes. I paused for a moment, and then said with a passionate voice, "Self-serving! This is completely different than any other thing, including being gay, because this is external. I have put my life to the Rotary four-way test *bigger* than *any of you* have ever done! This is a four-way test speech, and you let students, members, etc., come give speeches about the four-way test. This is *no* different."

The room was in shock—I was *never* a person who raised their voice. It was quiet for a minute until one of the members who was an attorney mentioned that he had given speeches to businesses to talk about LGBTQIA+ law that businesses are required to follow. He then mentioned he could give a speech about that.

The board was open to that.

"Can I give my speech after that?" I asked.

It was quiet for a moment, and then the board agreed I could.

When I left that board meeting, not only was I physically tired, I was frustrated, mentally tired, and relieved. The plan was still on.

Changing My Name

I was a little frustrated back when I told my HR Director I was preparing to come out, she said, "For regulatory legal reasons, we are not able to change the name on your business card until it is legally changed." You see, my career entailed a lot of networking. I handed out at least one business card almost every day.

Following that conversation, I refused to hand out business cards with my former name on them. I had not planned on changing my name legally until later in the year, but I realized I knew exactly who I was: *I was Jennifer, and there was no going back.* What I was preparing to do, in a very conservative field, was *huge*. If I'd had any doubts about who I was, I would not have come out. I recognized the risks, but to deny who I was seemed riskier.

One of my counselors had mentioned a local law firm that offered a special program where they will take care of all the paperwork and represent you pro bono for your legal-name change. All you must do is pay the court's costs. You do have a few hoops to jump through in order to be accepted into this program, however.

I was sure that this was for those who normally could not afford legal services, which would not apply to me—but this firm considered all applicants, regardless of income level.

I reached out immediately, and after sending in my application, I was accepted two weeks later. My name was legally changed two days before I was going to come out very publicly. Now after they finished the legal name change, I was going to have to do the work to change my driver's license, passport, social security, bank accounts, credit cards, utilities, and a lot more, but I was still thrilled! The legal heavy-lifting was already taken care of for me.

Four Days Left

I want to share my journal entry from Oct 1, 2023, four days before my coming-out day. I am sharing this so you can see exactly where I was:

Today's the first day of the month I come out from hiding to share Jenn with the world. I'm not scared at all. I'm ready to just live. But that doesn't come without its challenges.

One challenge that I was in no way prepared for was how emotional I would be about getting rid of my guy clothes. I'm sitting here with tears in my eyes, not because I have any doubts, but because I have such a deep respect for what he did to get me to this point. He lived a great life, but nothing was ever settled within me. I have had a lot of happy moments in my life, but I never smiled like I do when I get to be Jenn. It's just this natural smile that is in no way forced, and when I tell the story of my life to people, my euphoria skyrockets the second I start talking. No matter who I am talking with or how much they agree with who I am, this natural huge smile comes across my face, and nothing can take it away.

I've also had these very euphoric moments several times with people in my life when they will call me Jenn or use my she/her pronouns, even when I'm presenting male. Every time this happens, this same huge smile comes across my face, and I have zero doubts this is who I am supposed to be.

I was blind carbon copied on an email this last week that made my day. A client had reached out to my boss and said they had not heard from their new representative. My boss sent the following response:

"You will have a new representative assigned to you effective October 13th. I can have her reach out as soon as that gets done. Will that work?"

Her . . . when I saw those three letters I was filled with natural, internal joy and I felt like I was floating. This is a dream, but I'm so happy, I don't want to wake up.

Two days later the judge approved my legal name change. I was finally legally Jenn!

The next day I wrote: *Tomorrow everyone in all my circles will know I am Jenn, and I am so ready!*

Chapter Eleven

Coming Out

Hi, I'm here today because being here at our Rotary Club is one of the most important and rewarding parts of my life. I have immense respect for this club, and all the valuable relationships I have built with all of you, and I care deeply about serving our community here alongside you. If you don't know me already, I joined the club over three years ago and I've served in a variety of ways such as the AV Team Lead managing the computer and microphone in our meetings, Director of Public Relations, and serving on the Board. I have met some of my closest friends here, and I am grateful for your friendships.

However, over the last several years, I've been going through an enormous personal journey. But the time has come where my personal journey has fully transformed, and I need to be able to be completely authentic about my life. I need to be honest and transparent with my close friends, my community, and certainly all of you.

So, I'm here to introduce myself to you now officially. I am a proud transgender woman and I'm ready to start living as my true self in our community.

For all of you out there that have your own opinions about LGBT, it's important to know until early 2021, I was not supportive of LGBT issues, and did not have empathy with LGBT struggles. Honestly, I am ashamed to say I wasn't accepting until I realized I was part of it.

I'm here today to let you know that I'll be rejoining the club next week as my true self, Jenn. If I'm honest, I've been Jenn since I was four years old, although I didn't truly understand it. This has been about a thirty-three-year journey of self-awareness. In the past few years, I have secretly been in therapy working through a lot trying to understand myself.

I realized I was lying to myself, but my true self came out whether I wanted her to or not. In the last couple years, I ended up with stress induced kidney stones and shingles because my body could not handle the struggle of trying to suppress my own reality. The happy person I am was fading quickly and I was spiraling toward depression. I have been living a lie so deep for my entire life, that I've only recently been able to acknowledge it myself. This struggle has been so overwhelming that I physically, mentally and emotionally cannot survive another year without allowing this transition to happen.

I recently came out to family and friends who luckily have all responded with love and support. I am grateful to have started with an employer this year who's very accepting and is helping me live my truth with clients and colleagues. My Pastor at my church has been open and loving, and these gifts of acceptance are truly life changing.

To all of you who don't know the real me, it has been killing me to not tell you. It has been especially difficult in Rotary Club meetings where we say the four-way test. Before I decided to come out, I put it to the four-way test.

First, is it the truth? It is absolutely the truth. I wouldn't put myself through all of this and the more challenging life I could have because of this if it weren't the absolute truth. I have navigated changing my birth certificate, my legal name, public bathrooms, the judgment of strangers, and laws that may be implemented that will interfere with my personal freedom. For me, these risks are worth the truth.

Second, is it fair to all concerned? I think it's fair to most. I pray that this will not affect my children's lives, but I also don't think it's fair that they don't know the real me. And I teach my kids to be proud of who they are, so I need to live that with action. It's fair to my friends and colleagues because all of you deserve the respect of knowing the authentic version of who you're talking with.

Third, will it build goodwill and better friendships?

If you give me a chance, I really believe it will. Honestly, it already has with the people I have shared my story with in-person and the thousands of people that I connect with online. As part of my journey, I began an anonymous Instagram page a couple years ago which I used to help release my thoughts. I wrote out and shared the story of my journey, and support has flooded me. I now have over 18,000 followers, which is something I didn't expect or even try to achieve. But so many people have reached out to me to share how my story has helped them feel less alone because their story is similar to mine. This silver lining gives me hope that I can continue to help others in their journey, as I continue through mine.

Fourth, will it be beneficial to all concerned? I know for me personally it's beneficial for me to be my true self. I will be happier and healthier without hiding who I am. Will it be beneficial to you? I hope you will find that having someone like me in your life will add more compassion and humanity to understanding something so complicated. If you have questions, I would love the opportunity to sit down over a cup of coffee with you. It doesn't matter whether or not you agree with my understanding of who I am. All I hope for is that we can move forward with mutual respect and authenticity.

Please please do not tiptoe around me. My name is Jennifer, but my friends call me Jenn. My pronouns are easy: she/her, and hopefully after a little bit of awkwardness it will feel natural.

To all of you out there that don't understand, that's okay. It took me time too. 33 years, to be exact. It's all so new to you. I'm sharing this with you because starting next week you will see me as Jenn. I understand it may take a little time but hopefully eventually the newness will wear off and you will learn to treat me just as you do any other woman so I can be a beneficial member of the club.

Thank you for your time. I'm looking forward to my future. I hope you are interested in being part of it.

The response from being bold and being me paid off. I gave that coming out speech in "guy mode" (or whatever guy was left) in front of about 100 business-people. I was a little nervous, but when I stood in front of that room, all my confident feminine energy took over. I delivered that speech with certainty and assuredness. When I was done, the room erupted in a standing ovation. No one said anything negative. Several people came up to congratulate me and express their support.

If you want to watch me give that speech, it is on my website Jennspire.com and just click on the "About Jenn" button at the top of the page.

I also sent a written copy of that speech out in an email to hundreds of people, as many people as I had email addresses for, and posted on my other socials. I received a lot of great responses of support.

I share this to let you know there is still faith in humanity!

https://www.jennspire.com/comingout

Stepping Back Into That Room

After I came out, I took off work for a week to transform. I got my first feminine haircut and highlights, had my eyebrows waxed and colored, had my first mani-pedi, had my first professional photoshoot as Jenn, and even had a professional do my hair and makeup for the shoot, had my first counseling session as Jenn, had my first vocal therapy presenting as my true self, and changed my driver's license.

On the seventh day after I gave that speech, I stepped back into that room as promised, as my true self. I got up early to take my time with my makeup and curl my hair. I put on my new favorite blue dress, along with my cute matching necklace and earrings, slipped my feet in my favorite comfortable beige three-inch strappy heels and I was off.

I walked in the door as I had done the previous week, and just like the previous week, a lot of people said "Hi" to me. The only thing different was now they were saying "Hi Jenn." Sure, I got some looks, especially from the older generation, but many of these people had not seen a trans woman, or at least not that they are aware of. Also, I was 6'5" with my three-inch heels. I stood out, and I owned it!

It was a great day. These people gave me a standing ovation the week prior when I gave a speech telling them who I really was, and it was evident that when I showed up that day that they meant it. They were going to accept me, or at least try their best to do so.

https://www.jennspire.com/34-comingout-steppingbackintothatroom

The Call I Didn't Want

One of the worst possible things happened to me after I stepped back into that room, or at least that is what I thought immediately when it happened.

When I came out to my parents, one of their biggest fears was that I would lose my job when I came out publicly. I always said it would not happen because of how I was going about this. One of the things I was doing was creating numerous allies at work. People were extremely supportive of me, which is why when I was called into work on my day off, I never thought anything of it. I never anticipated they would lay me off. But they did.

I should have seen it coming as we had an all-new leadership team since I came on board six months prior. The new leadership decided we were overstaffed and laid off forty of us that day. It was suspicious that they did this the day before I was going to start work as my true self.

When I was told the news I started crying and said, "Really, you're laying off the trans woman? Do you know how difficult it is going to be for me to get a job without a business track record as Jenn, one that proves I'm still good at my job?" You could see it in their voices and faces that they truly did not want this either, but this was an executive-level decision that was beyond them.

I still questioned the motive of the executive team and thought the timing was suspicious. I quickly realized in the end that it doesn't really matter. Before I left there that day with my car loaded with boxes of my personal things from my office, I had a smile on my face. I knew right then and there that God had way bigger things planned for my life, and now I was going to go find out what they were! I was excited about the future—a little nervous, but excited!

https://www.jennspire.com/35-comingout-thecallididntwant

Counseling, Part II

Back to Counselor #4 . . . (And yes, I have ADHD and that is okay. It is also part of who I am, and I am proud of it because it is just how my mind works.)

After I accepted myself as a transgender woman, but before I started HRT, I asked my counselor a question: "Do you think I am trans?"

"Why does it matter what I think?" she asked. "What matters is how you feel inside."

Initially, I was frustrated with this answer. In some ways, I wanted validation that I was on the right path, but I realized she was right. It was not important what anyone else thought. What was important was how *I* felt, and I was confident in that.

The next time we met, after I started HRT, I told her, "I finally feel like Jenn. Please call me Jenn and use my pronouns of she/her."

That day, we made it official. She changed my name and pronouns in her notes, she started calling me Jenn, and it felt right. There are a few other things I want to share with you from my sessions with Counselor #4 that are important to my story.

After the end of December 2022, I told her: "Everything has flipped for me. Now I feel like wearing my male clothes is like dress-up. It feels like a costume. That, in itself, feels more like how it should be."

One session out of the blue, as I was telling her about all of the good things that had happened, and she challenged me. "Make sure you deal with the loss of marriage," she explained. "I know you have feelings of betrayal. It's good to have a reality check every once in a while."

I took some time to think about this during the session, and after. I did spend a little more time dealing with the loss, but as I told her in the session, "I will spend more time doing that, but I feel mostly at peace with that. I grieved the loss of my marriage for the many months I was having those extremely difficult conversations. I knew in my heart that she was never going to be able to understand and support me the way I needed her to. I just so badly wanted to be wrong, because I was so in love with her. I moved on and found peace in myself as we were pulling apart."

A little bit further into the conversation I realized, "It's kind of hard, because it's obvious we both still care about each other. We laugh about the kids at night and sometimes watch TV together and talk about it. It's like nothing has changed, but it has."

My counselor responded, "There's an expiration date on those times." I knew she was right. She said, "You evolved, and she didn't. Sometimes it's better to end a relationship than stay in it, especially with someone who says they're never going to change. That's not healthy."

February 7, 2023, was the first counseling session when I wore a bra and panties. I told her about it, and she asked how it made me feel. I told her, "Never before in my life did underdressing feel right, but now with where I am with all of the estrogen coursing through my body, it feels right. I am also pretending to be *him* now. That feels right, too."

In another session, we talked about independence. Growing up, I was very dependent on my parents, particularly my mother. After working through some of this, I realized that I moved from being dependent on my mother to being dependent on my ex and her parents, to finally being independent on my own . . . and I loved it!

In our final session, we wrapped up some loose ends. I told her, "Things are going well with me. I'm in a good place. I have a job that I love, with people who love me, and tools to take with me that can help me when I need to pick myself back up occasionally." We wrapped things up talking about my journey and how I used to refer to myself as my "former name" side and my "Jenn" side. I so badly wanted to make that dual gender life work, because then maybe I could have it all. It was never going to work, however, because that life was never the life I was supposed to live.

"Maybe you created the two sides as a defense mechanism," she suggested. "You know, to not have to deal with one's self, the one *true* self, because that is scary. The unknown is scary, and you were just defending yourself."

I went back to see her once, to check-in the week after I came out, but I realized during that session there was nothing negative to work through. I was in a good place.

The Golf Tournament

I did not do much for the following three weeks after I was laid off, except help plan a golf tournament. It was for one of the non-profits on which I serve as a board member, so I was on the planning committee for this event.

The day of the golf tournament was a fun and surprisingly euphoric day. It was literally so cold we moved back the time of the golf tournament by a couple hours, but I didn't know that. The email telling us that went to my old email, and I had been moving everyone to my new email because the old one had my former name in it. So, I ended up being the first one there. While I waited for others to arrive, I helped the director unload her car and then ran to Starbucks to pick up the coffee they donated for our tournament.

When I arrived with the coffee, there were a lot of people around. No one batted an eye at my 6'2" self walking in. After we set up the coffee, I sat down to help with registration checking golfers in.

Not a single person looked at me funny, or even gave me a second glance.

After the golfers teed off, I spent most of the day driving around on the golf cart with one of the thirty-year-old volunteers, chatting and asking golfers if we could take their trash; that way, they had more room on their carts when the beer cart came around. The volunteer and I chatted about everything. One point in the day, I mentioned something about being trans. She did not care at all, but like many people in my life, she had never talked personally with a trans person.

We talked about everything, and I got to teach her a lot, which had become one of my new favorite things to do. At one point, I mentioned how nice people had been to me all day. She said, "I don't think they even know. Until you told me, I did not know or did not even think about it." I was floored! I always had hoped I would be able to "pass" as a woman by my birthday in March, but I *never* considered I would start passing less than a month after I fully came out publicly! What an amazing feeling that gave me! It was not that passing was important, but it was very affirming.

I acknowledge that I was very blessed! I was born with a lot of softer feminine features, which as a kid always got me picked on. These features always made me look a lot younger than I was. Early in my childhood I hated this but being the optimistic person I have always been, I always said to myself, "I know looking young will benefit me someday." I never imagined how much I would be grateful for those feminine features one day.

The Gala

I had been attending formal events my entire life. Whether it was weddings or galas for my work or the organizations I volunteered for, I had always spent most of my time at these events watching the ladies in their beautiful dresses picking out the dress I wanted to be wearing. I dreamed of wearing a beautiful dress to an event a multitude of times.

Within a matter of weeks after coming out, my dream came true. My friend invited me to be a guest at her table for a large nonprofit gala. I was ecstatic! I did not want to break the bank for a one-night event without having a job, so I found a beautiful long black dress on Amazon.

It was a night I will always remember. I talked to so many people that knew me before and everyone was incredible!

https://www.jennspire.com/36-comingout-thegala

An Unexpected Day

It was just a typical Thursday, then out of the blue my friend Bill called and asked, "Are you available? I need you here to help me with something." When Bill called, I did my best to be there, especially because he was one of my biggest supporters and did so much for me. I told him, "I'll be there in fifteen minutes."

I pulled up to the building and walked in. It was an art gallery full of local photographs. Bill was holding the wheelchair of his mentor's wife with his mentor in the wheelchair next to him. You see, this couple was living in the nursing home. The husband stopped taking care of himself and they thought they were going to lose him. Bill saw this happening, and started to visit them more often and take them out of the nursing home to do fun things. His health immediately started improving!

As I walked in, they were all moving through the art exhibit with a guide who was explaining the photographs. As I joined them, Bill asked me to take over and push the wife's wheelchair, so he could take pictures of the couple to remember this day. I immediately grabbed the wheelchair. We spent the next half an hour admiring the photographs and learning the backstory behind each of them. It was a great experience and many of the photographs drew emotion, just looking at them.

And then we came to the last photograph. It was taken in the 1980s. It was of a row of little girls on a church pew all dressed in their little Sunday dresses and Mary Jane shoes. And then *déjà vu* hit me like a brick full of emotion. I remembered the hundreds of times watching my mother, my sister, other girls and ladies at church wearing their beautiful dresses. *I wanted to be them.* I wanted to be wearing those beautiful dresses to church, but I knew I could not ever share these thoughts with anyone. I did not want to find out what would happen if they knew.

https://www.jennspire.com/37-comingout-anunexpectedday

Chapter Twelve

More Firsts

I had gone through so many firsts to get to this point, and now that I was here, I realized the firsts were just beginning:

First Thanksgiving

It was just about like every other Thanksgiving, except the getting ready part. During the holidays, I typically tried to wear something mostly casual until my ex said, "You are going to wear *that?*" So I would change into something a little nicer, typically a button-up shirt with jeans.

This Thanksgiving, I decided I was wearing a dress—because I had always wanted to wear one for the holidays. I applied my makeup, curled my hair, took some pics, and I was off.

I arrived and it was just a normal Thanksgiving except everyone said, "Hi Jenn!" They also commented on my cute dress.

"You are brave to be wearing heels," the ladies said.

"These are just like wearing sandals," I smiled.

We had delicious food and great conversations. It was a wonderful first Thanksgiving!

The next day was my cousin's annual Friendsgiving. I had been invited for years but had never gotten to go, because my ex and my family never got along; as a result we did not go to "extra events"—but now I was free to be close to my family. I made sure to make time for this.

I am outgoing now, but it was not always that way, so there are times when I may walk in a room where everyone knows each other and immediately, I am more reserved. This was one of those days. I greeted my cousin and her husband and said "Hi" to the two other family members who were there. I made small talk with a few people and then I sat down at a table with one of my family members.

This person had the best intentions and I love them a lot, but in introducing me, I was outed—they had said I used to be a guy. I had walked into the party as the tall girl, but now everyone knew I was the one that was different. Since I embraced my true self, I have never cared what some random stranger thought of me or my decision to transition, but these were people that I would see again, at least at future parties. I froze when this happened, but it kind of turned out to be the best thing, in some respects. It switched my thinking from, "Do they know [I'm transgender]?" to me going into my teaching mode, explaining all types of things.

Some trans people do not like talking about it. Not me. I love any opportunity where I can teach people about this complicated, beautiful life that is being transgender. No one was weird after that, either, and the women embraced me. Another great evening with amazing people!

https://www.jennspire.com/38-morefirsts-firstthanksgiving

Vocal Therapy

Three months before my coming-out date, I began taking steps to work on my voice. I had recently reached out to my doctor at the gender clinic about doing some voice therapy. They referred me to the Ear Nose and Throat practice at their hospital.

I walked into the office in guy mode, and they used my name "Jenn." This was the first practice in person that used my name, and while I was a little nervous I might know someone around there, I loved every second of it.

They called me back and confirmed what I wanted to be called and my pronouns. I told them I preferred she/her, but if someone messes it up, it's not a big deal for me as I am presenting male and I'm very easy about it. Then they asked why I'm here. I explained that I'm very forward-facing in my organization, so everyone will be looking at me when I come out. I want my presentation and voice to be spot-on, as I'll be under a lot of scrutiny. I also explained that a few months after I come out, I want the random person on the street to just *see* and *hear* a woman. If I want to share I'm trans with new people, I can . . . but that will be my choice. They understood.

Next, they took out the scope. First, the nurse shot this stuff up both nostrils that tasted terrible and then left me. She told me they do this to numb my nose and throat, because they are going to use a scope. I never anticipated this, but to be honest, I had no idea what to expect.

They stuck a scope up my nostril and my eyes watered and I coughed as it went up through my nostril and down my throat. When they got it down there, I was asked to say certain things, cough, hold a certain note, etc. Next, they brought out the scope and the doctor showed me what my vocal cords look like, that they were in good shape and working well, that there was a little bit of mucus which can be from allergies (which I had and later in the year, started on allergy shots, so I could have a clear throat to project my feminine voice) and from not drinking enough fluids. She recommended I drink more water, which I told her I would try to do even more of.

She explained that voice feminization can be done two ways. One is through voice therapy and the other is through vocal surgery, but even with vocal surgery, she recommended voice therapy; surgery can only change pitch, which is only one of the parts of voice feminization. She explained that her goal is for women to achieve their desired outcome through voice therapy and hopefully, they would not need vocal surgery.

She asked me if I was interested in vocal surgery. I told her I wanted to focus entirely on voice therapy, because I wanted to avoid having surgery on something so important as my vocal cords. She explained what her vocal surgery method was like, just the same, in case I changed my mind. She also explained the process that she uses to shave the trachea, if that was bothering me. That interested me, so I kept that in the back of my mind.

I began vocal therapy the next month. It was a unique process. My vocal therapist explained that we were going to train my voice, in a similar way that a singer trains theirs. She recorded what my current voice was like, and we began to push the pitch higher through a series of repetitive exercises I still do to this day.

As I was progressing and getting into my feminine voice more, she told me she was surprised. She told me the next step she likes to work on is inflection at the end of words, but I was already doing it! It just came natural to me. We continued to work a few more sessions, mostly on those same exercises and then on reading passages slower and inflecting my voice in the right places. It was hard work, but hard work pays off.

First Surgery

I had been on HRT for less than a year, and while the results vary with each person, it had done more for me than I ever imagined. The changes I was experiencing caused me to hold off on any facial feminization surgeries for the time being, maybe for good.

For a long time, what bothered me was my Adam's apple. Other people told me that they did not notice it, but I did. It had always bothered me when I was presenting as female. Since it always bothered me, I had tracheal shave surgery to remove it. I went to a local hospital and had the same Ear, Nose and Throat doctor I had previously seen do the procedure. She is a pro, as she has done so many of these.

On the day of the surgery, I drove over to my parents' house. Mom then drove me to the hospital. She and I waited for hours while we waited to get in and then while I had the procedure. Gosh, I love Mom! After I was through all the intake, I put on the hospital gown and waited hours in bed with Mom by my side for my doctor to get out of her emergency surgery. When the specialist showed up, I asked how much she expected to shave off. She replied, "One to three millimeters."

The surgery went really well! I was pretty drugged up, so I only caught pieces of what the specialist said back in my hospital room afterward. I remember her saying they didn't use stitches, just glue that would come off naturally. "Don't scrub it in the shower," she advised. And she mentioned painkillers that I would have for four days. It was a good thing Mom was there to catch the rest.

Mom picked up my medicine from the pharmacy while I was in surgery and drove us to my house where I just wanted to lay in bed all weekend and cuddle with my pup! Mom is the absolute best! Not only did she do all the things I already mentioned, but she also insisted that she stay the first night, just in case I needed anything. Mom and Dad also stopped by multiple times throughout the weekend to check-in and bring me food.

A couple weeks later, I had my follow-up appointment. My doctor agreed it had healed nicely. I told her I was thrilled with the results and complimented her on her skills, especially when I asked her, "How much do you think you shaved off?" She replied, "About four millimeters." I believed it! I was so happy and glad I did it!

https://www.jennspire.com/39-morefirsts-firstsurgery

A Special Moment

One day in late January 2024, I had a great night. I had a wonderful time networking with people, like I normally do, but that wasn't the best thing that happened.

Let me go back several months to catch you up first . . . one of the things I did before I came out was meet with some LGBTQIA+ business owners for support in the business community. At one of those first meetings, the owner's new employee was there. She had just moved here, and the main reason was to be near the awesome godfather of her kid because she needed support. You see, within the last few months before we met, her child told her that he was a boy—not a girl. This mother, although supportive of our LGBTQIA+ community, found it was very difficult when it came to her doorstep with her child, as I am sure it is for many.

When we met, this mother was stressed and worried about a lot of things. That day, I encouraged her to ask me anything—and she asked me a lot of hard questions. We also talked about how she might be able to support her child. As we left, I told her to reach out to me anytime.

This mother, whom I had not seen since that day the previous year, came up to me at the event and said,

> Our conversation we had that day meant the world to me and changed our lives. I went home that day and wanted to be more supportive of my kid. I told them that day if they want to present as a male full time that they are welcome to do so. He has been presenting male ever since, and is so much happier. You are amazing, and I just wanted you to know how much you mean to me.

Hearing these words, I was filled with an enormous amount of joy! Just talking to someone for an hour I got to change the lives of a family. What an amazing feeling and a moment I will never forget.

Reunion of Friends

A couple days before the holidays, most of our friends from high school were home and had a chance to meet up. Our group dynamic had not changed a bit and didn't stop a beat, as we reunited for the first time in many years.

It was fun to catch up and see how different our lives are now. In some ways we're all very different, but in so many ways we are the same. As you might expect, my life had changed the most! I came out to each of them privately before I officially came out to the world. All were extremely supportive, and all continue to be very supportive of me living as my true self.

As we were chatting about old times and new, one of them said something I will never forget. "I don't think we really ever really believed you were a boy . . . we didn't even call you by your first name." It was such an interesting comment that made all the sense in the world.

https://www.jennspire.com/40-morefirsts-reunionoffriends

First Christmas

Growing up, I always thought it was funny that my Precious Moments "Baby's First Christmas" ornament was a girl. I never imagined that one day it would be my favorite ornament. The funnier part was that for years Mom didn't realize it was a girl.

When Mom gifted that ornament to me the Christmas after I moved out, a huge smile appeared on my face. Sometimes, ornaments hold more surprises than we think!

Christmas was not much different than it normally was, except it was my first one as Jenn. Everyone treated me the same, and it was a great day. The only thing that stuck out in my mind was how nice it was to finally receive the type of cute gifts that I always wanted.

New Year, New Me

My divorce was settled the morning after New Year's Day, less than an hour before we were to see the judge. I got 50/50 custody, like I wanted, and I was so pleased with it all! It was such a relief and a huge weight off my shoulders! My top priority and challenge had been my ongoing concern about losing joint custody of my children. Now, that was no longer an issue!

I reflected about how I got there. As I looked back on that part of my journey, I realized I needed to come out before the divorce was final, and I was so glad I did. Coming out and living my life showed the world around me that I was still a great parent, and nothing had changed that.

It was a perfect way to begin the new year! New Year! New Me!

https://www.jennspire.com/41-morefirsts-newyearnewme

Letter to My Ex-Wife

Now that our divorce is final, I wanted to write a letter to you. I do not expect one in return.

As I transferred all our family memories to the enclosed flash drive, I had a lot of emotions. I teared up a lot, not at what is lost, but at what we had. Most people like me reject their previous life. Not me. I will always cherish it.We had a lot of great moments together that I will always remember.

I will also never look at you in any negative way.While it hurt that the one I loved was not able to accept any part of the real me, I respect that. I know it was never part of your journey. It was mine. Before I left that house (which the only reason I did was because you had made it clear you would never be able to be with me) I so desperately wanted to tell you I regret hurting you but was scared to for legal reasons. Never in a million years did I ever think I would do that and for that I am deeply sorry. But also, never in a million years did I think I would transition.

As I really tried to share with you several times when I was figuring things out, I have been dealing with a lot of gender issues my whole life. I just never understood them. I know in hindsight that I really should have done the work to figure me out before I brought you into this, and for that I am truly sorry. I never ever even imagined in my wildest dreams that I was trans, but that was my defense mechanism. I remember looking at trans people even in the past few years before I started transitioning and thinking, "That must be hard to feel like you were born in the wrong body . . . I'm glad that's not me."

I never meant to hurt you or your family, and I hate that me not figuring things out sooner ended up doing just that. In the past few months before I moved out, you asked where things were going, and I wanted to tell you so badly because you were always my best friend, but when things changed between us, it didn't feel safe to tell you anything.

I wrote a letter I wanted to read you in family counseling, but for legal reasons I didn't want it in writing while our divorce was ongoing, so I'll share a revised portion of it with you now:

I started on hormones near the end of 2022 before I moved out. I started on a low dose because I wanted to know if I would feel right in my body before I made any changes with us (because you had made it clear you would never accept me as a woman), knowing it would likely end up with one of us filing for divorce. It didn't take but a couple weeks and I felt right in my body for the first time in my life.

I continued to take them and hide the physical changes from the world the best that I possibly could. I know you think that I didn't consider the kids. Figuring out how to deal with this with the kids was always my top priority!

For months I did a ton of research and was talking with other trans women who have done this with kids, and I came up with a plan. The thing I was told by all of them was with young kids you don't need to define who you are. Just slowly introduce them to it, letting them see. And even when they ask, "Daddy, are you a girl?" just say, "What do you think?" and then, "Okay, if that's what you think." So that's kind of the approach I took, but even more watered down.

Since I moved out, I extremely slowly started showing a little bit of who I am to the kids . . . it started with my pink and gold design of my house, then I started wearing a little more girly pjs, and the only other thing I did until I told them with you, they saw my painted toenails. The research and *conversations I did all told me at the accepting ages our kids are, it will be much easier for them if you just let them be and you don't need to define anything. Our kids will continue to be okay if we just let them be, so that's exactly what I always tried to do.*

My plan was to continue slowly doing these things until I was ready to come out, while I refined my appearance and showed my worth at my job where I was valued. I knew my team would be supportive when I told them because that's the kind of people that I worked with. They're all good people. Everything was going well and then they laid off forty of us in one day. I should have seen it coming with all new leadership, but they laid off basically everyone that had been there less than two years.

I know our family looks different than we expected, but we are still a family. I was looking forward to counseling with you and beginning that honest communication for our amazing kids. If you ever want to try that, please let me know.

I do not expect your friendship that we always promised each other, even in divorce. I know that you have shut the door on that, but know that I will always cherish the moments we had, and my door is always open.

Sincerely,

J

Back to Life

About three months after I came out, I was having a bit of a down day. Getting things accomplished typically helps start to break me out of it, so I was washing the dishes.

As I frequently did, while I was doing chores around the house, I was listening to music. This particular day, I was listening to Christian music. I was busy doing dishes when a song called "Good Plans" came on. This was the first time I had heard this song. I immediately fell in love with it. The song talks about how I have been through a lot, but I know He (God) has good plans for me. Nothing will stand against me because He has good plans for me. That song was powerful and then the next one came on.

The next song was called "Back to Life." In the song it says, "You brought me back to life." And a little bit further into the song it says, "The enemy thought he had me, but Jesus said you're mine!" I started tearing up and felt the power of these songs.

I know it's very common within my LGBTQIA+ community that if you are a Christian that you turn away from God when you come out, because of the hateful weaponization of the Bible that often occurs within many churches and people that call themselves Christians.

In fact, it is so common that I had a lot of people, including counselors, who repeatedly asked me if my relationship with God is the same. I know they expected me to say that I was stepping away from that life, but each time I told them, "No, it's stronger. I can feel that God has great plans for my life. I cannot say for certain whether or not He made me this way, but I can say I am confident that He is using me for some big plans of his. I feel this strong pull to change this world for the better. For me, that's a God thing."

He brought me back to life to be part of his big plans of helping people understand and healing individuals and families. I could not wait to see exactly how He was going to continue to use me.

First School Event

Early in 2024, my kids' school was having a winter dance, and my kids wanted to go. I was nervous. This was the first time I was going to present as the real me at a very public event at their school. I was so nervous; that is, until I got ready. As I curled my hair and did my makeup, this calm came over me. I looked in the mirror and said, "Jenn, you've got this!"

When we arrived at their school, I walked into the building full of confidence. I received a lot of looks, not even necessarily because I am trans, but because of how I was dressed. (Side note to my trans sisters: sometimes people just notice you, and trans has nothing to do with it.) My daughter wanted me to dress up and wear a dress, so I did.

I felt like most of the looks were because I was a tall, well-dressed woman and about the only parent dressed up. No one seemed to care, or at least care enough, to say anything to me. It was all worth it, and I would not take back a thing, because near the end of the night my daughter ran over to me with a boy that she liked and introduced me saying, "This is my Mom!" I want to point out that I have never told my kids to call me "Mom" or refer to me as their mom, but my heart smiles every time and the joy radiates from me!

https://www.jennspire.com/42-morefirsts-firstschoolevent

A Special Moment with Dad

Dad and I have always bonded over beer since I became legal. We would always be sharing the latest beer that we loved and thought the other should try. Even more fun than that, for the last few years we had been attending brewery festivals to try beers from all over the country. It was such a fun bonding experience, and one I had hoped would continue after I transitioned.

When Dad offered to buy my sister and me tickets to the upcoming brewery festival, I was more than thrilled! It showed he was not ready to give up on our special relationship, and it meant the world!

The date was all set, and we were going to meet my cousin and her husband, and my aunt and uncle there. It was going to be great. The date ended up getting moved back, but my family was all wanting to get together to enjoy some beer. We made our own little brewery tour and walked between several small breweries. It was a special time with my family, but that was not the most special part.

My favorite part of the entire day occurred on the drive downtown. My dad started to get emotional. "I want to have a serious conversation," he said, which made me *nervous*. "I want to apologize to you. I know I have not been supportive of you enough. I wanted to tell you that last week Mom and I talked to our pastor, who was really supportive of us and you, and then I told my men's group through church this week as well. People just embraced me, and it was amazing."

I was so thrilled to hear this. I had heard for months that Dad was struggling, but he was always very loving when I saw him, so I did not see this. When he told me that he was no longer hiding me from others, I got a little emotional. It was exactly what I wanted, and I knew in time he would come around if I just gave him time.

https://www.jennspire.com/43-morefirsts-aspecialmomentwithdad

Job Hunting

After I lost my job, I did not have energy to pursue another job for a while, so I did not do much. For a few weeks, I just enjoyed life. After that I started applying for jobs. Even though I had a great resume, I was not getting interviews.

After a couple months of that, I made some changes to my job hunting and process and started getting calls from recruiters. They found me some jobs I could interview for. Some jobs fit my skills well while others were a stretch.

My name had been legally changed and I was happy with my feminine voice, so the only indicator that I was transgender was if an HR form had a place for previous legal names. The other challenges I experienced being in interviews was keeping my gender-specific language straight, and sharing without oversharing in a way that it would give me away.

I was building my confidence through each interview and I was improving with each interview. It never went anywhere beyond a first interview, and it had nothing to do with me being trans. Being in the conservative field I was in, these hiring managers would have flinched at a trans woman coming in the door. There was no flinch. They had no idea I was transgender. That really built my confidence, but shortly after that, I realized my heart was not there anymore. It was *here!*

In early March 2024, I realized that I did not want to have any kind of a traditional job anymore. I knew exactly what I wanted to do, and I decided to invest my time, money, and resources into my passion and making it happen! I was going to start Jennspire!

First Birthday

My first birthday after I came out was special. I celebrated with my family the previous week, as my mother and sister were going to be out of town. Celebrating with them was great. My kids were even with me.

After I took the kids to an Easter egg hunt for my church, we went and had lunch with my parents and sister at my childhood favorite Mexican restaurant. Afterward, we went back to their house. It was great opening up the type of gifts I always wanted to open, but the big moment that made me a little emotional came after this.

After the presents, it was time for cake. Mom searched and found a candle, then lit the candle and they all started singing "Happy Birthday." As they were singing, I could feel it coming, and I couldn't help but be filled with joy. They were about to say my name and when they sang "Happy Birthday to Jenn," a big smile appeared on my face. A great birthday!

The day of my actual birthday was also a day to remember. It started with a very special coffee. I met up with a fellow author I was introduced to through a mutual friend. She was excited about the book I had just recently started writing, and gave me all kinds of tips.

I went home and immediately continued working on my book, implementing her advice. You might be asking yourself why I was working on my birthday when I didn't need to? This was my passion. It gave me energy, and my conversation that morning really fired me up to write all day.

I wrote until it was time to go celebrate. My friend Ash and I met up at a local bar that was having a Trans Day of Visibility celebration and had a beautiful time. We saw some good speeches, drag, contests, and had some great conversations.

https://www.jennspire.com/44-morefirsts-firstbirthday

First Easter

My first Easter as my true self was special and one I will never forget!

Easter has always been special to me because I am a proud Christian, but it has always been confusing for me, too. Since I was little, I would watch women and young girls wear pretty dresses to church, just like that photograph of all the young girls sitting on the church pew that brought back so many memories. Even my mother and my sister wore them for Easter and I remember them matching. They were so beautiful, and I remember always wanting to be part of it. I wanted to wear a pretty dress, have my hair curled and wear fancy shoes! I wanted to match them! I had no idea why, but I knew I wanted more than anything I wanted to look like them!

On Easter 2024, I made my wish come true! I wore a pretty dress, curled my hair and wore fancy shoes! It was an amazing time! Since my mom and sister were out of town, it was just Dad and me. He was going to accompany me to my church.

I arrived that morning at my parent's house for Dad and me to ride together. When he saw me, the first thing he said to me was, "That's a pretty dress." I was finally in an Easter dress like I always wanted to wear, and my dad was complimenting me!

We arrived at church, and I introduced Dad to my amazing pastor. She was thrilled to meet him, and Dad told me he was glad he got to meet her.

After church, Dad and I went and had a special brunch, just the two of us! It was amazing food with amazing company! It really was an Easter to remember!

https://www.jennspire.com/45-morefirsts-firsteaster

Chapter 13

Full Circle: Letting It *All* Go

In April 2024, I joined a group I never thought I would be part of. It was a group about growing your confidence and getting out of your own way to do amazing things. Something that was different for me is it involved quite a bit of Reiki and holistic practices, things I hadn't ever opened my mind up to before.

The evening of the solar eclipse we did a new moon reset. We completed a series of exercises. In the last exercise, we reflected on our dreams. I realized that night I rarely remember any dreams from my sleep and the only ones I ever could remember are the ones that reflected a desire to feel like the woman I am today. This started opening my mind up to try other things. The next was breathwork.

Toward the end of April, I did Somatic Breathwork for the first time. I do not think I was sure if any of this was real, but I quickly learned it is! As I was going through the session laying on my couch on my back with a sleep mask on and eyes closed, I was just breathing at first, but as the music picked up speed and my breathing became more intense and deeper I started to feel more. Then the instructor said to take a deep breath in as far as you possibly can and hold it. She asked a series of questions and then she said, "What have you been telling yourself, or allowing others to make you feel?" I burst into sobbing tears, those same hardcore tears that came when I finally surrendered, stopped fighting, and *accepted* being transgender. These tears I was experiencing were a result of everything I have been through in my life. As I went into the portion of deep belly breathing where I breathed into every ounce of my body and then breathed out of all doubt, first my hands started trembling and then my whole body was shaking violently, and I was sobbing. I have had people my entire life telling me I'm not good enough for one reason or another and I thought I had moved past all of "it," but I realized that night, I had not. I had just buried it deep down. That night I cast away all self-doubt, any doubt about my Jennspire business I was creating, this book that I was writing, and I found the peace and calm I needed.

For any Christians reading this who think that doesn't sound normal or liken it to some kind of witchcraft or something, you should know I was speaking to God throughout and I was encouraged to do so. I filled myself with the positive light that I needed to move forward with everything with full confidence. It really was a mind-blowing experience that will always remind me to keep my mind open to new ideas, new methods, and new ways of thinking . . . because that is *growth*, and growing and evolving is exactly how I want to live my life.

My Wedding Dress

As I have mentioned multiple times in sharing my story with you, wearing a wedding dress was always a big dream of mine and an important part of my story. That day in 2022, I felt compelled to make that dream come true the best that I could, so I bought a wedding dress.

As I also mentioned, it was so difficult to not be able to wear it in the way I wanted to. Right before I moved out, I put it on during one of the opportunities I had when everyone was out of the house and while somewhat fun, it never felt right. I wanted everything to be more real. I think in the end, *I* wanted to be more real. I wanted *my life* to be more real, and *feel* more real in my body. After a year of electrolysis hair removal on my face, and over a year of HRT feminizing my body, I felt that it was finally the time to make this dream come true.

I made it happen after I came home from Easter. I was loving my makeup, and thought this was the perfect time, since I had a few hours before I had to pick up my kids. I went to my closet and prepared everything on my bed, except hanging my big wedding dress on the outside of my closet. First, I touched up my makeup and hair. This was the first time I wore a wedding dress with my real hair, so I wanted it to be perfect.

Everything was ready, so I slipped the dress over my head and wiggled until I could get it down over me. As it slid down over me, I looked in the mirror and started to smile big. I continued to get the dress all pulled down and laid all the layers of tulle down properly, and then reached around to work on the corset back. I had practiced putting a corset on myself many times, so I knew what I was doing, but this was different. This was more challenging, and took a lot more effort and time to get it laced in a way that it hugged me enough for the dress to stay up on me.

Next, I put on the bridal earrings I had been dying to wear but had not been able to wear the previous time as they were for pierced ears. They dangled so beautifully from my ears.

Next, I clipped my beautiful bridal necklace around the back of my neck and laid it beautifully above my now fully round B cup chest, and clipped the matching bracelet around my wrist.

Next, I sat down on the bed and slipped on my size thirteen ivory kitten heels I had purchased to go with the dress. I remember being disappointed when I bought them, because they were the largest size I could find in bridal shoes and my feet were so crammed in them they hurt. Now, after a year and a half of HRT modifying my body, they fit perfectly! That made me smile.

I then stepped up to my full-length mirror and I could not take my eyes away from the woman that was staring back at me. I felt beautiful, more beautiful than I had ever felt! I had always wanted everything in my life to feel real, and for the first time, it finally did!

https://www.jennspire.com/46-fullcircle-myweddingdress

Putting the Pieces Together

I want to conclude this story with something you probably do not know about me . . . I love mystery! I am talking about the new murder mystery movies and TV shows. I am always trying to figure out who did it, but the truth is I don't really want to guess correctly. I always thought it came back to loving the element of surprise. It may come from the fun that I have when I am being surprised, but I wonder if it runs deeper than that.

The truth is I have always loved being surprised. You will have to look hard to find someone who loves being surprised at their presents more than me. I get super excited. I always have. Mom always stored and wrapped our presents in the back room in the basement. I always knew exactly where they were, but I never looked once.

I have learned that many women love watching true crime mysteries. I do not like them; I never have. But the element of surprise that comes from opening a present or watching a new murder mystery movie or TV show, I cannot get enough.

Lately in my life, I have started to analyze everything. And this was just the latest piece, but it may be the biggest. The more I think about it, I wonder if my love of mystery and surprises also stems from my true identity and the struggles I faced to get to where I am today.

You see, even at a very young age, I knew I was different. I expect that deep down I probably knew why. I was really a woman, but saying that would sound crazy, especially after I was told it "wasn't funny anymore." So, I buried it deep down inside, and used crossdressing to fill that hole. But it never could really fill it—not fully. I think deep down, I always knew the answer, but throughout the years I was too scared of what that answer would mean. So even when I had a counselor after my mom caught me, I never told that counselor any part of the real reason I was there. I knew the answer, but I was too afraid to admit it to myself.

My only regret in life is bringing my ex into this without finding the answer. But again, I didn't *want* the answer—not back then, anyway. I do not think the world was ready for me in those days, and I would have been miserable. My young world was already miserable enough as it was, or at least many of my younger school years were. If I was not being picked on, I was sitting at home without friends. Why? Because I was different from all the other kids. It was obvious. I never acted like the boys do. I was an easy target. I can only imagine how much worse it would have been if they knew that I was a trans girl.

Life—and very likely, my Creator—shielded me from this, and helped me bury this deep, so that I might have the life I had and one day share my story with you.

I believe in fate. I always have. But maybe for me fate is not about finding that perfect predetermined person to spend my life with. Maybe it has always been about finding myself. When I found "her," I held her tight and never let her go because she makes me happier than my wildest dreams. Like I said, maybe it's not about finding that right person at all, or maybe now that I found myself that is the next thing coming, only time will tell . . .

As I have said many times since I started my journey to uncover who I really am, I don't know exactly where my life is going, but I'm excited to find out!

https://www.jennspire.com/47-fullcircle-puttingthepiecestogether

Jennspire

As I referenced throughout my story, I believe I was created in a very specific way for a very specific purpose. I wrote the following in my journal on March 3, 2024:

Lately, I have been feeling my life leading to something big. I've just had this feeling I am meant to do something that will change the lives of thousands if not millions of people. I have felt that God has been preparing me my whole life for this.

And then it happened . . .

Sitting in church today our pastor told us to open our hands palms up and just let God speak to us. When I did that, I could hear the voice of God say, "This is why I created you," and then I could see me standing on a stage speaking to a large audience. I just burst into tears. Until lately with the confidence I now have, speaking in front of even a small group of people terrified me. God is telling me that I need to prepare to be vulnerable in front of thousands and I am calm about it. I know what I need to do, I just need to figure out how I'll get there. But I know I won't do it alone. I have a huge support system. From my friends, family and most importantly my creator, I have all the support I need.

I was to be a motivational speaker/ coach. I was going to stop job-hunting and create a small business offering:

- Gender identity coaching services for family members of trans people to help them understand us better and have better relationships;
- Coaching services for others who are lost on their gender identity journey to find their peace, whatever that looks like for them; and
- Keynote/speaking services to organizations and groups of people about my journey to create understanding and inclusion.

I was going to use all my life experiences that had been leading up this, and do something I am passionate about . . . making a huge difference in people's lives and moving our cause forward—not by being louder than the haters, but by educating people that we are not something to be feared, and that we really are not that different from everyone else. We just want to be treated with respect.

A year or so ago, someone asked me a question in a question-and-answer session on Instagram and I said, "I am going to change the world." I never realized how much I was going to do this, but I could feel it was going to happen.

Coming out here in this conservative bubble I live in, I have already started a lot of conversations at people's dinner tables and had difficult, important conversations where I have educated numerous people.

I never thought I would be an entrepreneur and start my own business, but being Jenn has pushed me completely to an amazing, beautiful world, more beautiful than I ever thought life could be. I was ready for it all!

Jennspire Specials for Buying My Book

For a list of all of my offerings, check out my website, Jennspire.com.

Gender Identity Coaching

Whether you are interested in one-on-one coaching in order to have a better relationship with someone who is transgender in your life, or you are looking to find and maintain your *gender equilibrium*.

You may be asking yourself, What is gender equilibrium? Gender equilibrium is a term I created which means the place on the gender spectrum where the individual finds the most peace within themself and their environment. Gender is a vast spectrum. I believe everyone has a different place on that spectrum where they find the most happiness.

I would love to meet with you . . . and you can "Ask Me Anything." Unlike typical sorts of personal and professional coaching, I am not looking to be your weekly coach, nor am I looking to be your counselor. I am using my strategic mind (I have an MBA)—along with everything I have learned throughout my journey and all of the research I have done—to hopefully help you achieve some, if not all, of your goals in two to four sessions.

Book Online at Jennspire.com today!

Use Promocode "ASKMEANYTHING" for 50 percent off your first coaching session.

https://www.jennspire.com/book-online

Jennspire Sisterhood

A community for all crossdressers, transgender women, gender-fluid people, dual gender/bigender people, etc., to safely express themselves and grow in who they are. In the Sisterhood, we are making great long-lasting connections, growing as our authentic selves, and having amazing online and in-person experiences!

Join Us Now!

Go to <u>Jennspire.com/JoinTheSisterhood</u> today

Use Promocode "JOINNOW" for 50 percent off your first three months.

<u>https://www.jennspire.com/jointhesisterhood</u>

Transition Mentoring

Are you reading this thinking, "I 100 percent know that I am transgender, and I am at a point in my life where I need to transition, but I am scared"?

I know exactly how you feel as I have been there. I would love to take you under my wing, helping guide you through every step of the journey. I will mentor you in a way that you can have the best chance at having great relationships with those you care about, helping you focus on what is important, helping you stay positive during this challenging time, and giving you the best chance at being as happy as possible as your true self. Transitioning is difficult: Mentally, emotionally, and physically, but it can also be very rewarding if the right steps are taken. I would love to lead you through this part of your journey.

Unlike my other coaching, this is better as pre-planned coaching, mostly because it saves you money. The more sessions, the larger the discount I can offer. If you are interested, please email me through the Contact link on my website. We will then set up a call to discuss what your goals are, how often and for how long you would like to meet, etc.

The best is yet to come!!!

https://www.jennspire.com/contact

Follow me on social media @luvjennifermarie for motivation and inspiration.

*If you enjoyed this book, I would love to hear from you and PLEASE leave a 5-star review on Amazon to increase the willingness of other readers to read this book!

Keep reading for Answers to Questions Everyone is too Afraid to Ask!

Chapter 14

Answers to Questions Everyone Is Too Afraid to Ask

I have had a lot of challenging, but great conversations; many people had questions that they always wanted to ask, but weren't sure what was appropriate. In most of these situations, they were curious, but didn't want to be disrespectful or didn't realize their curiosity could be offensive to some in my community.

By explaining to people that I was different in that they could not offend me, and there was no question that they could not ask, it opened an entirely new line of questions. I want to share some of those questions and my responses with you, because I believe you can't really understand until those difficult questions get answered.

I do want to clarify that *none* of these questions are appropriate to ask a transgender person, as all of them have the ability to stir up negative feelings. I have opened myself up to be the one person that you can ask anything, because for me, it's all about educating people so that they can understand and in turn, treat people with better respect. I am going to start off with one of my new favorite questions and then jump right into the hardest questions.

What is your favorite thing about being a woman?

I love being able to feel emotions deeper than I ever have in my entire life. I have always been a person that wears their heart on their sleeve. I have cried so many times in my life, including many times in front of others, which I have never been ashamed of. But something I have never had was feeling those emotions so deep that they touch every part of my soul. Some of my ability to do that now may be a result of feeling freer than ever to experience all the emotions and express them, but I believe even more of that is all the estrogen in my body. While many women have told me that they hate how emotional that they get, I love it when it happens to me. It makes me feel so right within my body and I can't get enough.

Do you want to have the surgery to remove your *****?

First, if you are ever having a conversation with a trans person, *please do not ask them about their parts.* They are private, and if they want to share with you, they will. They don't ask you about what is in your pants, so please don't ask them. But, as I told you, I am different in that I am not afraid to answer any question.

Everyone's personal answer would likely be different but here's mine:

Throughout my life, I do not recall experiencing any discomfort or dysphoria in regard to my equipment until I realized who I was. When I fully accepted and embraced being transgender, just naturally I didn't want to look at it or touch it and when possible, I avoided it. When that happened, I realized I wanted it *gone* and I will likely have it removed one day, but it is highly recommended, and sometimes required, to have laser or electrolysis *down there,* so that is another pain, figuratively and literally.

While I am on this topic though, I want to explain that being transgender does not mean you are going to have *the* surgery. Many are not able to afford it, as it is a *very* expensive surgical procedure. There are others who prefer the equipment that they were born with, for a variety of personal reasons. Each of us is different, and each of us is valid.

When are you going to have breast surgery/boob job?

The correct term is breast augmentation, and I do not think I am going to. People think that transgender women need to have surgery to have breasts. This is just not true. Some do need and/ or want it, while others don't. After being on HRT for about a year and a half, I already have a full *B* cup. I believe they will continue to grow, and they will reach a full *C* cup, and if they don't, I think I am fine with that, too.

Are men who date transgender women gay?

This is a common misconception, and one that men who are attracted to transgender women sometimes make themselves. Transgender women are women. Straight men are attracted to the feminine, so they are not gay. There are cases, like mine, where we tend to present more feminine than many cis women prefer to present themselves, which men tend to love. These men are not gay.

There are men who are attracted to trans women, specifically because of their equipment. These men are not gay; it is a fetish for them. I am not going to condemn anyone that is fetishizing me, but I am also not going to date them, either.

Do you ever have a moment or consider presenting in guy mode now?

This answer could be different per the individual, but here's my response:

This is something I had wondered about as well, before I experienced it. Although I had an emotional moment moving *his* clothes out of my closet, it had nothing to do with the clothes themselves. I have always looked at men's clothes as boring. There are very limited options, it was very challenging for me to style them differently, so I always just wore some kind of pants with some kind of button up, when I wasn't wearing a t-shirt, and even more importantly, they were not the pretty things I always wanted to be wearing.

Early in my transition, I did not want to think about wearing anything from my past life, but a few months into my transition, I began to experiment with different masculine clothing, but wearing it in a feminine way as many women do. But the idea of wearing a suit or tux, or worse, a tie. . . I never liked wearing one, and even the thought now of wearing one kind of makes me sick.

How do you justify being transgender is not a sin?

I struggled with this myself, at first. Not being supportive of the LGBTQIA+ community before 2021, I was also in the same boat, but I didn't do any biblical searching or research. Like many, I just listened to the hate I was being preached in church. I am not going to go into a philosophical discussion, because that is not what this book is, but here is my answer:

There is nothing in the Bible that says being transgender is a sin.

People who want to make the argument that God creates every one of us perfectly as man or woman want to ignore the fact that 1.7 percent of the population are born intersex[8]. If you do not know what intersex is, it means someone who is born with both parts, male and female. Also, in my case, I believe I was made perfectly, and transgender is part of that.

---

8. Amnesty International, "Intersex Rights," May 10, 2017, https://www.amnesty.org/en/latest/campaigns/2017/05/intersex-rights/#:~:text=An%20estimated%201.7%25%20of%20children,with%20variations%20of%20sex%20characteristics.

The best explanation that I have read was said by The Reverend Asher O'Callaghan, a transgender man[9]:

> In the beginning, God created day and night. But have you ever seen a sunset!?!? Well trans and non-binary people are kind of like that. Gorgeous. Full of a hundred shades of color you can't see in plain daylight or during the day.

> In the beginning God created land and sea. But have you ever seen a beach?!?! Well trans and non-binary people are kind of like that. Beautiful. A balanced oasis that's not quite like the ocean, nor quite like the land.

> In the beginning God created birds of the air and fish of the sea. But have you ever seen a flying fish, or a duck or a puffin that swims and flies, spending lots of time in the water and on the land!?!? Well trans and non-binary people are kind of like that. Full of life. A creative combination of characteristics that blows people's minds.

> In the beginning God also created male and female, in God's own image, God created them. So in the same way that God created realities in between, outside of, and beyond night and day, land and sea, or fish and birds, so God also created people with genders beyond male and female.

9. ProgressiveChristianity.org. 2023, "Beautiful Words From Asher Callahan," October 17, 2023, https://progressivechristianity.org/resource/beautiful-words-from-asher-callahan/.

Trans and non-binary and agender and intersex, God created us. All different sorts of people for all different sorts of relationships. Created from love to love and be loved. In God's image we live.

God is still creating you. You are no less beautiful and wild than a sunset or a beach or a puffin. You are loved. You have a place here.

And for me, maybe the most important, I know what I feel in my heart. I have a personal relationship with God, and I believe I am doing His work, just as He created me to do. I literally heard His voice tell me, "This is what I created you for." That's all the justification I need.

Would you give your child hormones if they told you they were transgender?

I do not know. I have not done the intense research to make that decision but what I know is if my child told me that they were transgender here is exactly what I would do:

1. Sit down and thank them for sharing this with me.
2. Discuss everything about why they feel this way.
3. Get them in therapy with someone who specializes in working with transgender children.
4. Let them experience therapy for a period, continually checking in and having conversations with my child.

5. We both would meet with a physician who specializes in working with transgender children. We would discuss and explore the idea of putting them on blockers. Each person has different thoughts on this, but I would be very likely to allow them to block the hormones that cause permanent changes to their body. This would give us more time to explore whether or not and when we might introduce HRT.

6. Talk to someone myself. People want to think that transgender people are thrilled to have a transgender child because they are like them. That is just not true. We know better than anyone the internal and external challenges that come with being transgender. We didn't choose this life and we wouldn't wish this on anyone, let alone our children. Also, like any parent, without knowing it, you dream up a life for your child that is typically very gender specific. When that dream is altered, it is important for the parent(s) to cope with it.

As I explained a little bit in my answer, I do not know whether I would put my child on HRT. There are a lot of factors in that decision, many of which I have not ever done the research on because it is not something I am currently dealing with. I do believe in using blockers, when needed, to be able to block permanent changes. While I will not say whether or not I believe I would put my child on HRT, I do know one thing for certain . . . It should *never* be up to anyone not involved in that specific child's life to make that decision. It should be up to the parents and the physician, because every case is different.

Do you think trans women should be allowed in women's sports?

Everyone has a different opinion about this very divisive topic. I'm also not going to debate this with anyone, but here's my opinion based on the facts that I have read:

Transgender people in sports are subject to all the regular drug testing that cis people are and then some. Transgender women must be on HRT for a specified period and maintain certain levels to be able to compete. I do not know that period of time, and I expect it varies according to the sport and level of competition.

People who want to point to the fact that our bodies are different because of the hormone levels we experienced before HRT refuse to consider that there are cis women that have higher testosterone levels than some men have. Should they also not be allowed to compete?

People also want to ignore what happens to our bodies from the HRT. My body, the first day on a low dose of HRT, had piercing pains and they still come and go. My body has lost so much muscle, and it is obvious whenever I do physical activity or lift something. My bones are more brittle. I get injured much easier than I ever did before.

People who want to point to the fact that I am 6'2" so I have an advantage, refuse to consider that there are many cis women who are taller than me. Should they not be allowed to compete? No one can prove that if I was born biologically female that I would not still have been as tall. There are all types of people whose bodies give them an advantage . . . take Michael Phelps, for example. Should he not have been allowed to compete because his body gave him a superior advantage?

Again, it's all my opinion, and it's not up for debate.

Why should transgender people be allowed in the bathroom of the gender they identify with?

There are very few issues that drive me up the wall, and this is one of them. There are several key points here:

1.   Transgender people are not perverts. When we go to the bathroom, all we want to do is get in and out. Honestly, most of us are more worried than you are. We are worried you are going to say something rude to us when all we are trying to do is pee.

2.   There are people that are perverts in both men's and women's restrooms. I do not send my kids into a bathroom alone, and neither should you.

3.   If bathroom bans were enforced, men would be beating up transgender women in the bathroom. Everyone deserves the right to safety, and no law should ever take anyone's safety away, when laws are supposed to be created to do the exact opposite.

4.   If bathroom bans were enforced, there would also be big, burly transgender men in the women's bathrooms. Do you *really* want them in bathrooms with your little girls?

If you were to date a woman now, what are you in terms of sexuality?

I am a woman, so if I dated a woman, I would be a lesbian, unless I am also into men, which, in that case, I would be bisexual.

What else should I know?

When you are talking about someone who is transgender, please refer to them as *transgender, trans, trans man, trans woman,* or *trans person,* and do not say, "transgenders" nor "a trans," as both are degrading.

If you see a person that you identify as transgender, please feel free to compliment them, just as you do any other person. It could make their day. But, *please* do not compliment them in a way that you are acknowledging they are trans. Even if it's done in a positive way, they likely do not want to feel othered, and your compliment could instead make them feel dysphoric.

How old is too old to transition?

I have been receiving this question a lot lately from older people who are wanting to transition, but are having doubts. If I was older, I might be asking myself the same question.

First, I never encourage anyone to transition. As a gender identity coach, I do my best to remain impartial. People know who they are, and like my counselor said, "Why does it matter what I think?"

But this question goes much deeper than caring if someone thinks you should transition; all of these individuals are all asking if they will be happy with the results of HRT at their age. This is up to each individual, what they feel inside and what their expectations are.

Anyone who is entering transition needs to manage their expectations. Every person's results are different. I'm not a scientist, but the older someone is, the more their body has undergone changes from puberty and aging as that gender. These changes become more challenging to reverse over time. In other words, the later in life one begins HRT, the less results one is likely to experience from taking the medications. If I had transitioned earlier, I would have had more physical results; in fact, some people think transitioning in their thirties, like I did, is too late. I am not going to state a cutoff. It's up to each individual.

If you have asked this question yourself, without telling you what you should do, I would love the opportunity to help you tap into your truth and help you find your *gender equilibrium. If you are ready to transition, I hope you will consider my mentorship program so I can help you live your best life!*

Now for me, starting HRT was not for the physical results. While I love the outward results that I have had, that was not my primary goal. My primary goal was to feel right inside and it did that for me in less than two weeks. Each individual needs to make that personal decision for themself. But, do I think it is ever too late for anyone to live as their true selves, assuming that they are realistically prepared for the results? No, I do not.

Epilogue

When I was growing up, I was worried about what every single person thought, so much that I got defensive when people were mean to me. When I realized who I really was and started taking steps to become her, who I was meant to be, all of that changed. I stopped caring about what everyone else thought and only about what I felt and knew was right for me.

To All of My Beautiful Gender Diverse Community:

Throughout my journey, I have never and will never look down on anyone in the gender spectrum and say anything negative about them because they do not transition. I had someone come at me when I was "crossdressing" because I was not "trans enough," and look at me now! For me, it's about finding that balance that is right for you.

If you are struggling with that balance, I would love the opportunity to help you find your *gender equilibrium* and help you maintain it.

I have friends that I refer to as trans, but not transitioning. For whatever reason they do not transition, they are still valid.

You are all valid! Be you, however is best for you! Ignore the noise!

I love you all!
Jenn

https://www.jennspire.com/contact

And last but certainly not least . . .

Follow me on social media @luvjennifermarie for motivation and inspiration.

*If you enjoyed this book, I would love to hear from you and PLEASE leave a 5-star review on Amazon to increase the willingness of other readers to read this book!

Made in the USA
Las Vegas, NV
13 October 2024

96757568R00159